GOD'S POWER TO
CHANGE
YOUR LIFE

Books by Rick Warren

The Purpose Driven® Life

The Purpose Driven® Church

Rick Warren's Bible Study Methods

What on Earth Am I Here For?

Living with Purpose Series

God's Answers to Life's Difficult Questions

God's Power to Change Your Life

LIVING WITH PURPOSE

RICK WARREN

GOD'S POWER TO CHANGE YOUR LIFE

ZONDERVAN®

GRAND RAPIDS, MICHIGAN 49530 USA

ZONDERVAN.COM/
AUTHORTRACKER

ZONDERVAN®

God's Power to Change Your Life
Copyright © 1990, 2006 by Rick Warren
Previously published as *The Power to Change Your Life*

Requests for information should be addressed to:

Zondervan, *Grand Rapids, Michigan 49530*

ISBN-13: 978-0-310-27303-5
ISBN-10: 0-310-27303-X

Interior design by Beth Shagene

Printed in the United States of America

To Amy, Joshua, and Matthew.
I am so proud of each of you.
My prayer is that your lives will
demonstrate the message of this book.

CONTENTS

Preface

What would you like to change about yourself? Would you like to be more confident or more relaxed? Perhaps you would like to be more outgoing, less anxious, or less fearful. Most of us are more than a little interested in changing because we realize there is always room for improvement.

We have probably even read some self-help books and tried to change, only to find ourselves slipping back to the way we don't want to be. So what are we to do?

This book is mainly about two things: where the power to change comes from, and what we want to be like after we change.

The bottom line is that Jesus Christ offers us the power we need to become what he wants us to be. This book unveils both of these truths as expressed in the Bible—specifically in the book of Galatians. There we read that the outgrowth of Christ's power is "love, joy, peace, patience, kindness, goodness, faithfulness, gentleness, and self-control" (Gal. 5:22–23). This is a challenging list. We probably have some of these qualities by nature; the rest—well, that's why we want to change.

The change doesn't come all at once. It may take time. But when we rely on God's power, we can change. My prayer is that in reading this book and thinking through these qualities, you will embrace the power Christ offers, shed those traits you really don't want, and become the person he—and you—desires you to be.

CHAPTER 1

THE POWER TO CHANGE YOUR LIFE

In the years I have been a pastor, the number one question I have been asked is, "Rick, why can't I change? I want to change—I really do. But I don't know how." Or sometimes a questioner will add instead, "But I don't have the power."

We go to seminars and conferences looking for a painless cure by which our lives can be zapped and changed by instant self-discipline. We go on diets. (I once went on a diet for an entire afternoon.) We join health clubs, and our enthusiasm runs strong for about two weeks. Then we fall back into the same old rut. We don't change. We read self-help books, yet the problem with self-help books is that they tell us *what* to do but can't give us the *power* to do it. They say things like, "Get rid of all your bad habits. Be positive; don't be negative." *But how?* Where do we get the power to change? How do we get our lives out of neutral? How do we break out of the mold we're in? The good news is, Christianity offers the power we need.

We Can Have Resurrection Power

The word *power* occurs fifty-seven times in the New Testament. It is used to describe the most powerful event that ever happened, an event that separated AD from BC—the resurrection of Jesus Christ from the dead. And that resurrection power is available to change your life!

The most important thing in life is *knowing* Christ and experiencing the *power* of his resurrection. Paul writes, "I want to know Christ and the power of his resurrection" (Phil. 3:10). In another letter he tells his readers, "I pray that you will begin to understand how incredibly great his power is to help those who believe him. It is that same mighty power that raised Christ from the dead and seated him in the place of honor at God's right hand in heaven" (Eph. 1:19–20 LB).

Paul uses the Greek word for power, *duna-mis*, which is the root of our word *dynamite*. So Paul is saying, "God wants to give you dynamite power that can change your life." Yes, the same power that raised Jesus Christ from the dead two thousand years ago is available to us right now to transform the weaknesses in our lives into strengths. The Bible describes resurrection power as the power to cancel our past, the power to conquer our problems, and the power to change our personality.

God's Power Will Cancel Our Past

First, resurrection power is *the power to cancel our past*—our failures, mistakes, sins, and regrets. When I say "cancel," I'm not talking about denying the past as if it never happened. *Cancel* means to eliminate, to neutralize, to offset something.

Have you ever gotten halfway through a project and wished you could start over? Suppose you are painting the living room, and you step back and look at the color that seemed perfect on the sample chart. On the wall, however, it doesn't look so perfect. You wish you could start over.

A lot of people feel that way about life: "I've made so many mistakes. I wish I could just wipe them out and start over." Failures, problems, bad decisions—we have all suffered from them. But some people just can't seem to let go of the past, and as a result, they let their past limit their present opportunities. They live in a constant state of regret, continually lamenting, "If only I hadn't done that" or "If only I had made these changes." They repeatedly second-guess themselves. And they are tormented by painful memories. "I blew it, and I'm going to be paying for it the rest of my life."

God says that it is unnecessary for us to go around with a heavy load of guilt, old hurts, and memories of mistakes. In Colossians 2:13–14 he says he has forgiven all our sins and canceled every record of the debt we had to pay. He did it by allowing Christ to be nailed to the cross.

Jesus Christ knows the things we have done wrong, but he did not come to rub them in. He came to rub them out. He did not come to condemn us; he came to change us. A clean slate is possible! Think in terms of my son's Etch A Sketch. If he makes a mess of a design or picture, all he has to do is flip it over to wipe the slate clean; then he can start all over again. The Bible says this is what God does with the mistakes we have made. When we come to him, he wipes the slate clean.

In Jeremiah 31:34 God says to the Israelites that he "will remember their sins no more." This has to be one of the most amazing statements in the Bible—that the God who made the world "forgets." When we come to him, admit our sins, and ask him to forgive us, he cancels our past. God *chooses* to forget our wrongs, our mistakes, our failures. That's good news! Even if we were to die tonight and stand before God in heaven, we could ask him about some sin we committed yesterday, and he would say, "What sin?" He has canceled our past and set us free to get on with the present.

Why God Can Cancel Your Past

What is the basis of this forgiveness?

When Jesus died, one of his last statements from the cross was, "It is finished" (John 19:30). That phrase consists of just one word in Greek, *tetelestai*, literally meaning "paid in full, canceled." It was the word merchants wrote on bills when they were "paid in full," and it was the word stamped on a document declaring that a prison sentence had been commuted. Jesus says this is

15

what he did on the cross. He paid the price in full for every sin we have ever committed. Romans 8:1 tells us, "Therefore, there is now no condemnation for those who are in Christ Jesus." Jesus was crucified on the cross so that we could stop crucifying ourselves. He was hung up for our hang-ups. That's good news!

The question is, if God forgets a sin the moment we confess it, don't you think we ought to forget it too? How long do you remember a bill you have paid? I forget my bills as soon as I have paid them. I don't worry about last month's electric bill. Likewise, since Christ has paid our bill in full, we don't need to think about it anymore.

Someone has said that when we give God all our mistakes and failures, he throws them into the deepest part of the sea. Then he puts up a sign that says No Fishing. He doesn't want us to keep dredging up our sins.

Paul says, "Forgetting what is behind … I press on toward the goal to win the prize for which God has called me heavenward in Christ Jesus" (Phil. 3:13–14). However, we can short-circuit God's power in our lives by not believing that God has truly forgiven us or by choosing not to forgive ourselves. God's power is the power to cancel our past.

God's Power Will Conquer Our Problems

God's power is also *the power to conquer our problems.* Everyone has problems. They come with living in a fallen world. If you don't think you have any problems, check your pulse. The only people who don't have problems are in cemeteries.

The real problem is what we do with our problems. Inevitably, we try to solve them with our own power. How do we know when we are trying to solve all our problems with our own strength? We are tired all the time! A man who was frustrated with his lack of power to conquer his problems summed it up when he said, "I'm sick and tired of being sick and tired." We get this way when we try to solve our problems on our own. God wants us to stop *trying* and start *trusting* him with our problems.

I have met hundreds of people who feel as if their lives are out of control. They tell me, "My life is out of control; I'm a victim of my circumstances. What can I do? I'm powerless. Just about the time I make ends meet, somebody moves the ends." When I ask them, "How are you doing?"

they respond, "I'm doing okay, *under* the circumstances." Well, what are they doing *under* them? Someone has said that circumstances are like a mattress: if you're on top, you rest easy, but if you get underneath, you suffocate! A lot of us are *under* our circumstances. Although we cannot always control them, we can control how we respond to them.

You might be saying, "But, Rick, you don't know all the problems I'm going through. I'm having a tough time." If so, I encourage you to take your focus off your problems and focus instead on God's promises.

Paul asks in Romans 8:35, "Who shall separate us from the love of Christ? Shall trouble or hardship or persecution or famine or nakedness or danger or sword?" He answers his question in verse 37: "No, in all these things we are more than conquerors through him who loved us." Do you know what a *conqueror* is? A conqueror is "one who overcomes by gaining control." And Paul says that we are "more than" conquerors. The Greek word declares that we are superconquerors and that we can have *overwhelming* victory. If we put our lives in God's hands and rely on the power of Christ's resurrection, nothing can devastate us. Nothing can swallow us up or destroy us. That's the message of the resurrection and the heart of the Good News.

No matter how dark a situation may be, God can turn it around. No matter how hopeless life seems, God brings hope. The same power that enabled Jesus Christ to rise from the dead allows us to rise above our problems.

Acts 4 records the first serious opposition to the apostles' preaching of the gospel in Jerusalem. When the authorities threatened them, the apostles banded together and prayed. Notice what they prayed for. They didn't ask God to stop the opposition but rather to give them supernatural boldness in the face of the opposition (v. 29). He did (v. 31).

God's Power Will Change Our Personality

Resurrection power enables us to cancel our past and conquer our problems, but that's not all it does. *Resurrection power also helps us change our personality.* What would you like to change about yourself, and how would you go about doing it? Or to put it another way: how would your spouse like you to change? Maybe that would be more revealing. One wife said her husband is "too temperamental"—90 percent temper and 10 percent mental!

How would you complete this sentence: "It's just like me to—"? It's just like me to *be late all the time*? It's just like me to *be unable to stay on a diet*? It's just like me to *put my foot in my mouth*? It's just like me to *blow up*, to *be depressed*, to *get angry*? I'm sure you are well aware of the parts of your personality you would change if you could.

GOD USES A PROCESS

God uses a two-step process to change us. The first step is explained in 2 Corinthians 5:17: "If anyone is in Christ, he is a new creation; the old has gone, the new has come!" The initial turning point is when we commit our lives to Christ. We are not the same anymore; a new life has begun. This is why the Bible calls that step being "born again." Being born again doesn't mean we are reincarnated; it simply means we get a chance to start over. It is not turning over a new leaf, but getting a new life, a fresh start. It is a new beginning with a big difference. We now have a new nature and the indwelling Holy Spirit. A set of "spiritual batteries" is included to provide the power! That makes all the difference in the world.

Being born again, like being born the first time, is only the beginning. It is followed by a lifelong process described in Romans 12:2. J. B. Phillips paraphrases the verse this way: "Don't let the world around you squeeze you into its own mould, but let God re-mould your minds from within, so that you may prove in practice that the plan of God for you is good, meets all his demands and moves towards the goal of true maturity."

In the next chapter, we will examine more specifically how God helps us change and the tools he uses. Then we will take a close look at how he changes us by producing in us the fruit of the Spirit as listed in Galatians 5:22–23. Each chapter will be devoted to one of these character qualities. When the Holy Spirit controls your life, he will produce in you nine positive characteristics: love, joy, peace, patience, kindness, goodness, faithfulness, gentleness, and self-control.

How many of the people you work with or live with exhibit these qualities? How many of the people you work with or live with would say these qualities describe you? The sad fact is that rather than loving others, we often are unloving. Rather than living joyously, we feel defeated, depressed, and discouraged. Rather than experiencing peace, we feel uptight and pressured. Rather than being patient, we are frustrated and irritated. Instead of showing kindness, it's every man for himself. Instead of modeling goodness, we often feel there is nothing good about ourselves. Instead of being faithful, we neglect our commitments. We are more likely to respond to others in anger or resentment than in gentleness. And instead of practicing self-control, we watch our lives falling apart.

These are the contrasts between letting the power of God work in our lives and relying on our own power. We must remember, however, that the fruit of the Spirit isn't something we work up. It's something that God produces in us when we fully trust him with our lives.

Don't Put It Off

Only one thing will keep you from changing and becoming the person you and God want you to be. It's not the devil. It's not other people. It's not circumstances. It's procrastination.

I meet many people who are getting ready to live but never do. "I'm aiming to change," they tell me. And I want to reply, "That's good, but when are you going to pull the trigger?"

Procrastination is fatal. One of these days I'm going to go to the dentist. One of these days I'm going to have that surgery I need. One of these days I'm going to spend more time with the family … get serious about being a Christian … become active in church … go after that dream. One of these days I'm going to get into shape. One of these days! More often than not, that day never comes.

Why Spend One More Night with the Frogs?

One of my favorite movies is *The Ten Commandments*. I love the scene where Charlton Heston, as Moses, extends his arms and the Red Sea parts so the Israelites can walk through. My family gets a kick out of my behavior every time I see *The Ten Commandments* because, for the next couple of weeks, I go around walking and talking like Yul Brynner, who portrays Pharaoh in the movie. When my kids ask me something, I reply, "So let it be written; so let it be done!"

A humorous fact about the events surrounding the Israelites' exodus from Egypt concerns the ten plagues God sent on the Egyptians. Each plague mocked a different Egyptian god. For instance, the Egyptians worshiped lice, so God sent them a lot of lice to worship. Then there was the plague of frogs. The Bible says there were frogs everywhere. I'm sure Mrs. Pharaoh put pressure on her husband to give in and get rid of the frogs.

Finally, Pharaoh summoned Moses and said, "All right, Moses, I give up." So Moses asked, "When do you want me to get rid of the frogs?" Now Pharaoh's answer was classic. He said, "Tomorrow." He must have been crazy! Why would anyone wait any longer to have the frogs removed?

There is a famous sermon based on this text called "One More Night with the Frogs." How would you like to spend one more night with the frogs? Why in the world would anyone put off a change that was going to be positive? We would have expected Pharaoh to say, "Get rid of the frogs right now!" But, no, he said, "Tomorrow."

You and I do this all the time. We procrastinate by putting off changes that we know will be good for us. Why? Maybe we are complacent. Maybe we are too lazy to change. Maybe we are afraid because we don't know what the changes will involve. Maybe we are too proud or just stubborn. Whatever the reason, we procrastinate.

The NASA space engineers tell us that most of the fuel used in a rocket launch is burned up in the first few seconds of lift-off. It takes tremendous energy and thrust to get the rocket off the launching pad. Once it's moving and headed for orbit, it requires much less fuel and is easier to control and direct. It has overcome inertia.

It is one thing for me to tell you that Jesus Christ can cancel your past, help you conquer the problems you are facing right now, and change your personality. But it is quite another matter for you to overcome inertia and actually let him begin to do it now! Although you may agree with everything I say, you may still wait and let Jesus help you "one of these days."

Jesus Christ has the power to make changes in your life now. He will give you the power to get started and the power to keep going. He will give you the power to break the chains of procrastination.

If you have been unable to let go of your past, Jesus Christ offers complete forgiveness. He can put your life back together again. You may feel like Humpty Dumpty, so fragmented that nothing can put you back together. But it is never too late to start over! You are never a failure until you give up.

Maybe you are overwhelmed by your problems. Jesus' resurrection reminds us that no situation is hopeless. Relax. Trust God. You don't have to be controlled by your circumstances. No problem is too big for God. He is still in the resurrection business. What are you waiting for? Right now you can say, "Jesus Christ, take my life. Take the good, the bad, and the ugly. Take every part of me." Open your heart to his love right now and let his transforming resurrection power become a reality in your life.

Putting Thoughts into Action

1. Think about what it means not only to forgive, but also to forget.
2. Identify a problem you have been procrastinating about and what your first step should be in dealing with it.

CHAPTER 2

GOD'S PART AND MY PART IN CHANGING ME

One of my fondest memories of growing up is my father's garden. It seemed my dad grew everything in his garden. In fact, he always grew enough to feed the entire neighborhood. When people would stop by our home for a visit, they would usually leave with a sack full of fresh vegetables and luscious fruit.

The kind of fruit my father grew is just one kind of fruit—*natural* fruit. There is also *biological* fruit, the offspring of animals and the children of people. Then there is *spiritual* fruit, and that is what God talks about in Galatians 5:22–23: "But the fruit of the Spirit is love, joy, peace, patience, kindness, goodness, faithfulness, gentleness and self-control." These nine qualities describe the character of a fruitful, productive Christian.

How do we get these character qualities? Obviously, God doesn't just zap us one day and all of a sudden these qualities materialize in our lives. He uses a process. In this chapter we will look at that process.

It's a Partnership

The apostle Paul describes the two-part process God uses in Philippians 2:12–13, where he first says, "Work out your salvation," and then turns around and says, "It is God who works in you." It sounds like a contradiction, doesn't it? But it isn't. It is a paradox. The British sage G. K. Chesterton describes a paradox as "truth standing on its head to get attention." Paul's writings contain many paradoxes.

The key to understanding this paradox is the little word *out* in verse 12. Notice that Paul doesn't say, "Work *for* your salvation." There's a big difference. To work *for* something means to earn it, to deserve it, to merit it. The Bible clearly teaches that salvation is not something we have to work for. It is a free gift of God's grace. Paul says,

"Work *out* your salvation." Paul is talking about a "spiritual workout."

What do you do in a physical workout? You develop or tone muscles that God has given you. To work out means to cultivate, to make the most of what you have been given. That is what Paul says here: Cultivate your spiritual life!

God has a part in our spiritual growth, and we also have a part. He provides the power, but we must flip the switch to turn the power on. Work out your salvation, for it is God who works in you.

Let's look first at God's part in this process and the tools he uses. Then we will look at our part and some choices we need to make.

THE TOOLS GOD USES

God Uses His Word

The first tool God uses in changing us is *the Bible*. Through Scripture he teaches us how to live. Second Timothy 3:16–17 tells us, "The whole Bible was given to us by inspiration from God and is useful to teach us what is true and to make us realize what is wrong in our lives; it straightens us out and helps us do what is right. It is God's way of making us well prepared at every point" (LB).

Has the Bible transformed your life? I heard about a converted cannibal on an island in the South Seas who was sitting by a large pot reading his Bible when an anthropologist wearing a pith helmet approached him and asked, "What are you doing?"

The native replied, "I'm reading the Bible."

The anthropologist scoffed and said, "Don't you know that modern, civilized man has rejected that book? It's nothing but a pack of lies. You shouldn't waste your time reading it."

The cannibal looked him over from head to toe and slowly replied, "Sir, if it weren't for this book, you'd be in that pot!" The Word of God had changed his life—and his appetite.

If you are serious about changing your life, you are going to have to get into the Bible. You need to read it, study it, memorize it, meditate on it, and apply it.

When people tell me their faith is weak, I ask them, "Are you reading your Bible regularly?"

"Not really."

"Are you studying the Bible?"

"Well, not exactly."

"Are you memorizing Scripture?"

"No."

"Well then, how do you expect your faith to grow?"

The Bible says, "Faith comes by hearing, and hearing by the word of God" (Rom. 10:17 NKJV).

God Uses His Spirit

The second tool God uses to change us is *the Holy Spirit*. When we commit ourselves to Christ, the Holy Spirit comes into our lives to empower and direct us (Rom. 8:9–11). The Spirit of God gives us new strength and vitality and the desire and power to do what is right. As the Spirit of the Lord works within us, we become more and more like him.

Now, whatever you learn from this chapter, remember this above all else: *God's number one purpose in your life is to make you like Jesus Christ.* The Spirit of God uses the Word of God to make the child of God more like the Son of God. And what is Jesus like? His life on earth embodied the ninefold fruit of the Spirit: love, joy, peace, patience, kindness, goodness, faithfulness, gentleness, and self-control.

God Uses Circumstances

God's ideal way of changing us is to have us read the Bible to find out how we should live and then depend on his indwelling Spirit to enable us to do it. Unfortunately, most of us are stubborn, and we don't change that easily. So God brings in a third tool to work on us—*circumstances.* Problems, pressures, heartaches, difficulties, and stress always get our attention. C. S. Lewis once said that "God whispers to us in our pleasure but He shouts to us in our pain."

In the Phillips translation, Romans 8:28–29 reads, "To those who love God, who are called according to his plan, everything that happens fits into a pattern for good. God ... chose them to bear the family likeness of his Son." Nothing can come into the life of a believer without the heavenly Father's permission; it must be "Father-filtered."

The interesting thing about how God uses circumstances is that the source of the circumstances makes no difference to him. We often bring problems on ourselves by faulty decisions, bad judgments, and sins. At other times our problems are caused by other people. Sometimes the devil causes things to happen to us as he did to Job. But God says the source of the circumstance is irrelevant. "I will still use it in your life," he says. "I will fit it into my pattern; I will fit it into my great plan for your life, to make you like Jesus Christ." So there is no circumstance in life from which we cannot learn if we'll just have the right attitude.

Proverbs 20:30 has some more good news: "Blows and wounds cleanse away evil, and beatings purge the inmost being." Perhaps you have experienced the truth of this verse. Sometimes it takes a painful experience to make us change our ways. In other words, we are not as likely to change when we see the light as when we feel the heat! Why? Because we change only when the fear of change is exceeded by our pain.

I wear shoes for comfort, not for style. A few years ago I had a pair of black shoes that I wore almost every day for over a year. Eventually the soles got holes in them, but the shoes were so comfortable I continued to wear them. I wouldn't cross my legs when sitting on a platform because I didn't want people in the congregation to see the holes. I knew I needed to buy new shoes, but I kept putting it off. Then it rained for an entire week. After four days of soggy socks, I became motivated to change and bought some new shoes. The first step in change is usually discomfort!

God speaks to us through the Bible and by the promptings of his Holy Spirit, but if he can't get our attention, he will also use circumstances. For example, the Bible says that we should be humble, and the Holy Spirit enables us to be humble. But if we don't humble ourselves, he will use circumstances to humble us.

God can use every situation in our lives for our growth. That is his part. So what is our part?

CHOICES THAT BRING CHANGE

We Must Choose Our Thoughts

Spiritual growth is not automatic. Change is a matter of choice. We can't just passively sit around doing nothing and expect to grow. We must make three choices if we really want to change.

First, *we must carefully choose what we think about.* Proverbs 4:23, in the *Good News Translation*, says, "Be careful how you think; your life is shaped by your thoughts." Someone once said, "You're not what you think you are, but what you think, you are." That is, if you are going to change your life, you have to change your thought patterns. Change always begins with new thinking.

How does a person become a Christian? By repenting. Repentance is often a misunderstood term. I used to think of it as a man standing on a street corner with a sign that says, "Turn or burn!" However, the Greek word for repentance is *metanoia*, and it means to change your mind or perspective. When I became a Christian, I changed my perspective on many things. Romans 12:2 says that we are transformed by the renewing of our minds — not by willpower.

The Bible teaches that the way we think determines the way we feel, and the way we feel determines the way we act. So if you want to change your actions, you have to go back to the source and change the way you think. Sometimes you may act resentful. Why? Because you feel resentful. Do you know why you feel resentful? Because you are thinking resentful thoughts. The same is true for anger and worry and many other kinds of destructive thought patterns.

What I Think	Determines	What I Feel	Determines	How I Act

Imagine you have a speedboat and the speedboat has an automatic pilot. The boat is heading east, and you decide you want to go west. You want to make a 180-degree turn. There are two ways to do that. The automatic pilot is heading the boat east, but you can grab the steering wheel and turn the boat around by sheer force. Now the boat is heading west, but the whole time that you're forcing it by willpower to go west, you are under tension. That's because the boat is naturally inclined to go the other way. You are tense and uptight, and soon you become tired. You know what happens then. You let go of the "wheel" and … you go off the diet, or you start smoking again, or you stop exercising, or you slip back into your old patterns of relating to your family. The truth is, trying to force yourself to change by sheer will-power seldom produces lasting results.

The other way to change the direction of your boat is to adjust the automatic pilot. Now, the "automatic pilot" in your life is your thoughts. Remember the question I asked in chapter 1? How did you finish the sentence "It's just like me to be _____"? Once you finish that sentence a few times, I will be able to tell you what the automatic pilot in your life is set on.

But you can be transformed by the renewing of your mind. Don't focus on your actions. Don't focus on your feelings. People often say, "I'm going to be more loving" or "I'm going to be happy if it kills me." But forcing a feeling doesn't work. Simply focus on changing your thoughts.

When you change your thoughts, you also change the way you feel. Stop thinking the thoughts that are getting you into trouble and start thinking thoughts that will get you where you want to go.

Jesus said, "You will know the truth, and the truth will set you free" (John 8:32). When you base your life on truth—when you live with the right kind of thoughts, not misconceptions or false beliefs, and you base your life on right thoughts out of God's Word—you will be set free. You will find your old habits, feelings, and actions falling away.

God gives us his Word, but we have to use it. We have to practice biblical meditation. When I use the word *meditation*, I am not talking about sitting in a yoga position and chanting "ommm." You don't need transcendental meditation or yoga or any of those other techniques based on Eastern religions. Stay away from them. Meditate on God's Word. Read through the book of Psalms and see how many times David speaks of meditating on God's Word.

In Psalm 1 we read, "Blessed is the man who does not walk in the counsel of the wicked or stand in the way of sinners or sit in the seat of mockers." In other words, that person doesn't get his input from the wrong sources. "But his delight is in the law of the LORD [the Bible], and on his law he *meditates* day and night." As a result, "He is like a tree planted by streams of water, which yields its *fruit* in season and whose leaf does not wither. Whatever he does prospers" (emphasis added).

God says that when we meditate on his Word day and night, we will bear fruit. We will be fruitful, productive people—people full of love, joy, peace, patience, and the rest of the fruit of the Spirit. He also says we will prosper. There are two great promises in Scripture about success; one of them is Psalm 1, and the other is Joshua 1:8. Both say that the key to success is meditating on God's Word.

What, then, does it mean to meditate on God's Word? If we look up the word *meditation* in a dictionary, we find that a synonym is the word *rumination*. Rumination is what a cow does when she chews her cud. A cow eats some grass, chews up all she can, then swallows it. It sits in one of her stomachs for a while, and then a little bit later she burps it up—with renewed flavor. The cow chews on it some more and swallows it again. This continues for all four stomachs. That's rumination. The cow is straining every ounce of nourishment from the grass.

Meditation is thought digestion. Meditation does not mean that you put your mind in neutral and think about nothing. Meditation is thinking seriously about what you are reading. You take one verse and ask, "What does this mean for my life?" Talk to yourself about it, and talk to God about it.

God is quite specific in telling us what to think about. Philippians 4:8 says we are to ponder eight different categories of things and, by implication, to avoid thinking about the opposite kinds of things. I suggest you take a few minutes right now to read this verse and think about it. Talk to God about it. This will be good practice in meditating on God's Word.

Colossians 3:16 says, "Let the word of Christ dwell in you richly." You need to spend regular time every day—a minimum of ten to fifteen minutes—in which you sit down and read a portion of the Bible and think about what you have just read. Then talk to the Lord about it in prayer. That is the starting point for your part in change. You can choose what you think about.

We Must Depend on His Spirit

We can also choose to depend on the Holy Spirit. The Bible says that God puts his Holy Spirit in us to give us power. All Christians have God's Spirit in their lives, but not all Christians have God's *power* in their lives. Jesus gives a beautiful illustration of this in John 15. He compares our spiritual life to a vine and its branches: "I am the vine, you are the branches. He who abides in Me, and I in him, bears much fruit; for without Me you can do nothing" (John 15:5 NKJV).

In this illustration the branch is totally dependent on the main vine; it cannot produce fruit by itself. Fruit growing is an inside job. If I went out in the spring and tied apples on the branches of a dead tree and then took my wife out and said, "Honey, look at our fruit tree," she would say, "You tied those things on." That is what it is like when a Christian says, "I'm going to tie on a bunch of fruit in my life—a little patience here, a little goodness there, a little self-control here. I'll do it on my own." It can't be done. Remember, the fruit Christians bear is the fruit of the *Spirit* and therefore must be grown within.

Now you might be saying, "How do I know whether I am abiding in Christ? How do I know if I am hooked to the vine? How do I know if I am depending on his Spirit?" Simple—look at your prayer life. Your prayers demonstrate your dependence on God.

What do you pray about? Whatever you pray about is what you are hooked into God about, what you are relying on him for. Whatever you don't pray about is what you are trying to do on your own. Prayer is the acid test.

The secret of depending on God's Spirit is to be incessantly in prayer. Pray about your decisions. Pray about your needs. Pray about your interests. Pray about your schedule. Pray about problems you are facing. Pray about people you are going to meet. Pray about purchases. Pray about everything. That is what it means to "abide"—to be aware that God is always with you, to practice his presence. As you pray, you will start to see the fruit of the Spirit developing in your life.

We Must Respond Wisely to Circumstances

In addition to choosing our thoughts and choosing to depend on God's Spirit, *we can also choose how we respond to the circumstances of our lives.* Viktor Frankl was one of the Jews sentenced to the Nazi concentration camp at Dachau. He says that while he was in the camp, the guards stripped him of everything. They took his identity. They took his wife. They took his family. They took his clothes. They even took his wedding ring. But there was one thing that no one could take from him. In a classic book he writes, "The last of human freedoms is the ability to choose one's attitude in a given set of circumstances."[1] The guards could not take from Frankl his freedom to choose his attitude.

We cannot control all the circumstances in our lives. We do not know what is going to happen tomorrow, or even today. We cannot control our circumstances, but we can control how we respond to them. We can control whether an experience makes us a bitter person or a better person. What matters in life is not so much what happens *to* us but what happens *in* us.

Paul talks about this in Romans 5:3–4. He says we can rejoice here and now, even in our trials and troubles, for they will produce perseverance in us and help us develop a mature character. We can rejoice in our problems, not just endure them, because we know that God is using them for our benefit. God even uses the problems we bring on ourselves.

God also uses the situations that others mean for bad in our lives. This is a lesson pictured in the life of Joseph as told in the Old Testament. Joseph was betrayed by his brothers and sold into slavery. Years later he said, "You intended to harm me, but God intended it for good" (Gen. 50:20). This holds true in your life. Maybe there is someone right now who is trying to hurt you. Don't worry. If you are a believer, if you have put your life in God's hands, God can use even such a painful situation for good. He will develop within you a mature character. And that is what the fruit of the Spirit is all about. God wants to produce the character of Christ in our lives because he knows that the more we become like him, the more fulfilled we will be.

When God created man, he made him "in his own image" (Gen. 1:27). That was God's original plan, and it has not changed. He wants to make us like himself—not gods, but godly. He does it by working on our character through his Word, through his Holy Spirit, and through circumstances. The Greek word for "character" in Romans 5:4 means "tested and proven reliable." It brings to mind the work of a blacksmith, describing something that has gone through the fire, has been beat on and beat up as on an anvil, but has stood the test.

Have you seen the luggage commercial that features a gorilla? A suitcase is shown going out on a conveyor belt at an airport, and instead of being picked up gently by a nice gentleman, it is manhandled by a gorilla. He hurls the luggage around the room, stomps on it, jumps on it, and throws it up in the air. Now, that luggage has character. It is reliable and stands the test. This week you may feel you have been beaten up at work or pushed around at home, but God can use even these kinds of situations for good in your life.

Here is a key truth: *God produces the fruit of the Spirit in us by allowing us to encounter situations and people with characteristics that are exactly the opposite of the fruit of the Spirit.*

Consider, for example, how God produces love in our lives. Loving lovely people or people just like us is easy. But to teach us real love, God puts some unlovely people around us. We learn real love by loving that cantankerous fellow at work or that pesky neighbor. God teaches us to love by letting us practice on the "unlovely."

The same is true for peace. Anyone can be at peace in calm situations; that does not take character. God teaches us about peace in the midst of total chaos, when everything is falling apart—the phone rings, the doorbell rings, something is boiling over on the stove, the baby is crying, and the dog bites the cat. That is a situation in which we can truly learn inner peace. God works that way for each fruit he is developing in us.

It Takes Time

One last point: *it takes time for fruit to ripen*. There is no such thing as instant maturity or instant spiritual growth. Time is essential. When you try to rush fruit, it doesn't taste as good. Have you ever eaten gassed tomatoes? That is what you purchase at the grocery store. If farmers picked ripe tomatoes and shipped them, they would get smashed on the way to market, so the farmers pick them green and spray carbon dioxide on them just before they go to market. That gas ripens green tomatoes into red very quickly. Now, there is nothing wrong with those tomatoes. But if you have ever eaten a vine-ripened tomato, there is no comparison. It takes time for fruit to ripen. And God is going to need time to ripen the spiritual fruit in your life.

You can begin by telling God right now that you want to be a productive, fruitful Christian, that you want to cooperate with his plan. Commit yourself to reading, studying, memorizing, and meditating on the Bible. Ask God to use his Word to change the way you think. Invite the Holy Spirit to have free rein in your life. Don't hold anything back. Pray and talk with him about everything. Accept your circumstances as a part of God's plan to change your life. Ask him to help you respond to difficult people and unpleasant situations as Jesus would. God wants to produce the fruit of the Spirit in your life. Will you cooperate with him in that life-changing process?

Putting Thoughts into Action

1. Give an example of how God led you recently to a decision or an action by communicating through his Spirit or his Word.
2. Why is attitude important in confronting and acting on difficult situations?

CHAPTER 3

BECOMING A MORE
LOVING PERSON

First Corinthians 13 ends with these familiar words: "And now these three remain: faith, hope and love. But the greatest of these is love." Love is also the first fruit of the Spirit mentioned in Galatians 5. But what exactly is love?

Love is probably the most misunderstood word in the world. Part of the problem is that we use this one word to describe many things. We water down its meaning by overuse. I love my wife. I love America. I love pizza. I love my dog. I love you. I would love to have my back rubbed. We use the word *love* in so many different ways that it has literally lost its meaning.

Giving or receiving love is difficult when we don't even understand what it is. So, first, we need to clear up a couple of popular misconceptions about love. Most people think love is a feeling—a sentimental knot in the stomach, a quiver in the liver, an ocean of emotion. True, love does produce feelings, but it is more than a feeling.

In a *Peanuts* cartoon, Charlie Brown and Linus are talking, and Linus says, "She was so cute. I used to see her in Sunday school every week. I used to just sit there and stare at her, and sometimes she'd smile at me. Now I hear she's switched churches."

Charlie Brown looks up and says, "That'll change your theology in a hurry!"

How often we rely on our feelings and let our feelings motivate us to do all kinds of things we might not normally do.

Another misconception is that love is uncontrollable. Have you ever said, "I *fell* in love"—as if you had tripped? We assume that love can't be controlled. "I can't help it if I'm in love." Or the opposite: "I can't help myself; I just don't love him anymore." We talk as if love is uncontrollable, but the Bible says love is controllable. In fact, Jesus *commands* that we love others. His words indicate that we do have control over whom we love and whom we do not love.

Love is at the core two things. First, it is a matter of choice. The Bible says, "Over all these virtues put on love, which binds them all together in perfect unity" (Col. 3:14). Notice those two little words "put on." Love is something we can choose to have. If it were a feeling, we could not command it. But we can command a choice, and love is a choice. It is controllable.

The Bible also says that love is a matter of conduct. Love is something we do—an action, not a feeling. The apostle John expressed it this way: "Let us not love with words or tongue but with actions and in truth" (1 John 3:18). Too often we love with words but not with actions. A young man said to his fiancée, "I love you so much, I would die for you, my love." She replied, "Oh, Harold, you're always saying that, but you never do it."

Love is more than words and more than feelings. The Greeks had four words to differentiate different types of love: *storge*, which means natural affection; *eros*, which means sexual attraction; *philia*, which means emotional affection or friendship; and *agape*, which means unconditional, giving, sacrificial love. When the Bible speaks of God's love for us and the kind of love we are to have for him and for other people, the word is always *agape*, signifying a commitment to act.

Do you know that it is possible to love someone you do not even like? Remember what I said in chapter 2—that for God to teach us to love, he puts us around some unlovely people. It is easy to love people who are kind and lovely, but if God is going to teach us to love, he will bring some hard-to-love people into our lives. The fact is, our lives are full of people we don't like. We do not like the way some people talk. We do not like the way some act. We do not like the way others dress. But most of all, we tend not to like people who do not like us.

Lady Astor, the first female member of the British House of Commons, did not like Winston Churchill. One time she told him, "Winston, if you were my husband, I'd put poison in your coffee."

Churchill replied, "Madam, if you were my wife, I'd drink it!"

If you were to think about it for sixty seconds, you could probably come up with a list of people you do not like. They would probably be people whom you have trouble getting along with. Everyone is hard to love some of the time—even you—but some people are hard to love at any time.

Jesus never demanded that we have a warm affection for everyone. He did not have warm emotions for the Pharisees. We don't have to *like* everyone (isn't that a relief?), but we do have to *love* them. So how do we do that?

The Bible tells us there are five steps we need to take to learn to love people. But before we look at them, I want you to picture in your mind the person whom you find hardest to love—an obnoxious relative, a troublesome neighbor, or a disagreeable coworker. How can you learn to love this kind of person? Here are the five steps.

EXPERIENCE GOD'S LOVE

First, before we can love others, we must *feel and understand how deeply God loves us*. Ephesians 3:17–18 says, "I pray that Christ will be more and more at home in your hearts, living within you as you trust in him. May your roots go down deep into the soil of God's marvelous love; and may you be able to *feel* and *understand*, as all God's children should, how long, how wide, how deep, and how high his love really is; and to *experience* this love for yourselves" (LB, emphasis added).

Circle the words *feel*, *understand*, and *experience* in that passage. God wants us to feel his love, and he wants us to understand his love. Why? First John 4:19 says that we love because God first loved us. Why is it important to feel loved by God? Because unloved people are often unloving people. When I do not feel genuinely loved, I do not feel like giving love. So first we have to experience God's love ourselves. Jesus said, "Love each other as I have loved you" (John 15:12). That is the model.

Forgive Your Enemies

The second step in learning to love others is *forgiving those who have hurt us*. Colossians 3:13 says, "Forgive whatever grievances you may have against one another. Forgive as the Lord forgave you." It is impossible to love anyone fully and at the same time resent someone else. I cannot really love my wife if I am still angry with my parents. I cannot love my child if I am still angry toward my brother. You cannot give total love when your heart is divided. And a bitter heart is a divided heart.

You may be thinking, "I can't love my spouse. He is a wonderful person, but I just can't love him." You are probably still reacting to your past and harboring resentment against someone. That is what is keeping you from loving your spouse. And that is not fair to your spouse.

Many people have a just cause for their anger. For example, I heard a news report on the radio that one out of every three women and one out of every seven men will be abused during their lifetime. But we have to let go of the past to get on with the present. To begin loving people today, we must close the door on the past. And that cannot happen without forgiveness! Forgive those who have hurt you — for your sake, not because they deserve it. Do it so your heart can be whole again. The people from your past cannot continue to hurt you today unless you allow them to hurt you by holding on to resentment against them.

Anytime you resent someone, you give that person a piece of your heart, a piece of your attention, a piece of your mind. Do you want that person to have that? No. So take it back by forgiving. Forgive those who hurt you. Instead of rehearsing that hurt over and over, release it.

THINK LOVING THOUGHTS

The next step in learning to love others is to *think loving thoughts*. God's Word reminds us, "Don't just think about your own affairs, but be interested in others, too, and in what they are doing. Your attitude should be the kind that was shown us by Jesus Christ" (Phil. 2:4–5 LB). What does it mean to think loving thoughts? It means we begin to focus on other people's needs, hurts, problems, desires, and goals, not just on our own. As the old saying goes, it is easier to understand someone else when we walk a mile in their moccasins. Hurt people hurt people. If someone is hurting you, that person is doing so because he or she is hurting. We need to look beyond people's faults and see their needs. Then we can learn to love.

Have you discovered that the most obnoxious people and the least lovable people are those who *need* love the most? The people we would rather ignore are the very ones who desperately need massive doses of love. Everyone needs love. If a person can't get love, he will strive for attention. And if he can't get positive attention, he will work at attracting negative attention. Subconsciously, he is saying, "I will be noticed, one way or another."

In chapter 2 we noted that our thoughts determine our emotions. We cannot change our feelings, but we can go in the back door and change our thoughts. When we change the way we think about someone, we will gradually change our feelings about that person. And if instead of thinking about a person's faults we begin to think about his or her needs, it will change the way we feel. Try it and see for yourself!

Act in Love

The fourth step in learning to love others is to *act in a loving way.* You say, "Rick, you're telling me to act lovingly toward someone I don't even like. I couldn't do that. I would be a hypocrite." No, that is called loving by faith. When you love by faith, you act yourself into a feeling.

This is an important truth: It is easier to act my way into a feeling than to feel my way into an action. If I act as if I'm enthusiastic, I will soon begin to feel enthusiastic. If I act as if I'm happy, before you know it I will feel happy. Try right now putting the biggest smile on your face that you can muster up; then make yourself laugh—really laugh inside. At first it will seem forced, but dig deep and create the body movement of laughter.

You will begin to feel happier. If we begin to act lovingly, we will soon feel loving.

Not only do our actions influence our emotions but, as I mentioned earlier, our thinking also influences the way we feel. We can attack feelings from either side—or better yet, from both sides.

Change Your Feelings Indirectly

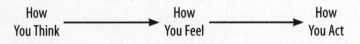

| How You Think | → | How You Feel | → | How You Act |

If you say, "I can't change my feelings," you are focusing directly on your feelings. You cannot change your feelings directly, but you can change them indirectly by changing your thoughts *and* your actions.

Now, how do we act in a loving way? Jesus gives us some help in Luke 6:27–28: "Love your enemies, do good to those who hate you, bless those who curse you, pray for those who mistreat you." He commands us to do four specific things.

First, Jesus tells us to *love our enemies*. How do we love someone who is hurting us? We must overlook his faults. Ephesians 4:2 says, "Be patient with each other, making allowance for each other's faults because of your love" (LB).

Then Jesus commands us to *do good*. How do we do good to people we don't even like? We look for ways to give to them. What can we do to serve them, meet their needs, help them, and benefit them? We can give. We can go the second mile. We can offer practical help. We can do them a favor. We can discover their needs and respond to them.

Jesus also says to *bless those who curse us*. What does he mean by that? He is referring to the way we talk *about* and talk *to* those who treat us badly. A blessing is a positive word spoken to or about others. We don't put them down; we lift them up. We encourage them. Proverbs 12:18 says, "The tongue of the wise brings healing."

Finally, Jesus commands us to *pray for those who mistreat us*. Praying for people will not only change them, but also change us. So how should we pray? We pray that God will bless people who are mistreating us, because the goodness of God leads to repentance. Perhaps God will bless these people so much that they will want to change. But even if they don't change right away, praying for them will change our attitude toward them.

What all this means is that love is an action. First Corinthians 13 says that love is patient, kind, and much more. Fifteen actions are listed in verses 4–8. When we act lovingly—when we are patient or gentle or kind—we are displaying the fruit of the Spirit. Love is not simply the first fruit mentioned; it is actually *the* fruit. All the other fruits are simply expressions of love. Love is patient. Love is kind. Love is joyful. Love is the basis of all positive actions.

To summarize: First you must understand that God loves you. Then you begin to feel it, not just intellectually but in your heart. Next, to free yourself of the past so you can love today, you forgive those who have hurt you. You then start thinking loving thoughts and acting in loving ways, and loving feelings will start coming.

Expect the Best

The last step in learning to love others may in some ways be the most difficult: *expect the best of even those you don't like*. First Corinthians 13:7 says, "If you love someone ... you will always believe in him, always expect the best of him" (LB). Love expects the best. Have you discovered that we tend to live up to what people expect of us? The father who always says to his son, "You will never amount to anything; you're just a dunce," is setting the boy up for failure.

When we expect the best, we bring out the best. This is loving by faith. And loving by faith is the greatest force in the world. Love is contagious, and it changes people. It can transform a personality!

You may be thinking, "Well, I would like to change my mate." Do you want to know how to do that? I can tell you the secret in one sentence. This is how you change anyone — your mate, your children, your mate, a coworker: *treat that person the way you want him or her to become.* Do you want your mate to succeed? Treat your mate as if he or she is a successful person. Do you want your children to be smart? Treat them as if they are intelligent, not stupid. Do not do this as an act of manipulation but because you genuinely believe in them. Love expects the best.

Experience God's Resurrection Power

You may be thinking, *Well, I am stuck in a marriage that is dead or dying. There's just no spark left. Once there was love, but now it's gone. Once there were feelings, but now they are gone.* Perhaps you have heard that painful statement, "I don't love you anymore." What do you do about that? Do you end the marriage? No, you ask God to resurrect those feelings of love.

The power that raised Jesus from the dead can also raise a dead relationship. How do you rekindle a lost love?

You can revive those feelings if you choose to have them. Saying "I am going to force myself to feel loving" won't work. You cannot force a feeling; you cannot force the spark back into a relationship. But you can attack the problem indirectly by thinking and acting lovingly. Your thoughts and actions will produce the loving feelings.

Christ spoke to the church at Ephesus about a love they had lost—their love for God. That love had become dry and passionless as they merely went through the motions of their commitment to him. Jesus told them to take three steps to rekindle that love. These steps may also be powerfully applied to the rekindling of our relationships. Jesus said, "*Remember* the height from which you have fallen! *Repent* and *do* the things you did at first" (Rev. 2:5, emphasis added).

The first step in resurrecting love is to *remember*. Rekindling love in your marriage starts with thinking about how you used to love your mate.

Remember the happy times. Recall the qualities that first captured your heart. Choose to remember the experiences you have shared—events that brought you close, such as dating experiences, things that happened early in your marriage, the birth of a child, or the purchase of your first home. Don't recall the bad things; those are easy to remember. Instead, choose to focus on the good things that have happened in your relationship.

The second step in resurrecting love is to *repent*. The word *repent* comes from the Greek word *metanoia*, which means to change your mind, to change the way you think. When Jesus calls you to repent, he is calling you to change the way you think about that person you have lost your love for. Stop fantasizing about what might have been. Stop daydreaming about what life might be like if you were married to someone else. Stop thinking about what life might be like if your mate were different or had done this or that. Stop torturing yourself with "what if—?" You are talking yourself into those unhappy feelings. Stop fantasizing and start thinking positive, truthful thoughts—the kind described in 1 Corinthians 13. If you want to rebuild a love in your life, memorize 1 Corinthians 13. Meditate on it and start acting on it.

Jesus' third step in resurrecting love is to *do the things you did at first.* Love takes action. You have to work at loving your mate—as hard and creatively as you did during your courtship and engagement. Do the things you did at the start. Perhaps you have not had a romantic evening in months—or years. It may be that you have not even had time alone together in months. Take time to go out on a date and do the things—buy the flowers, wear that special dress—that you did at first. Let your creativity come alive again.

Stop fantasizing about greener grass some-where else. The truth is that the grass is not greener on the other side of the fence; the grass is greener wherever you water it! If you will take the energy you spend complaining and fantasizing and invest it in improving your marriage, you will have a great marriage. You will rekindle those lost feelings no matter how long it has been since you last felt them. Love works if you work at it.

If you have the desire to resurrect a dying love, I want to challenge you to do two things. First, commit yourself totally to Jesus Christ. Frankly, I don't have much hope for marriages that are not based on a commitment to Jesus Christ. Human love is not strong enough to weather the storms of life. Human love dries up, but *agape*—God's love—never gives up.

The root of your problems is spiritual, not emotional or relational. Your relationship with God affects your relationship with your spouse and everyone else. When you are not right with God, you are not going to be right with other people either. The vertical and the horizontal planes must be in balance. Each affects the other. The starting point is to correct your vertical relationship with God, and then your horizontal relationship with others will be easier to correct. The Holy Spirit can fill you with new reservoirs of love you never thought you could have. You need God's love and power, so commit your life unreservedly to Jesus Christ.

The second challenge is to commit yourself totally to your mate, regardless of faults and flaws. Don't fall into the "I would love you if" syndrome: "I'd love you *if* you would do this or that for me." That is conditional love. God's love is the kind that says, "I love you, period. I love you unconditionally." Actually, God's love really says, "I love you in spite of ..." He tells us, "I love you in spite of your imperfections. I love you in spite of your problems. I love you." That is agape love, the kind of love that makes a difference.

So pray for a resurrection, and choose to do what Jesus says: remember, repent, and take action. When you do that, you will be surprised at how quickly your feelings return.

PUTTING THOUGHTS INTO ACTION

1. Think of an unlikable person in your life and a specific action you can take to show that you care about him or her.
2. Discuss how thoughts, feelings, and actions affect each other and what the outcome should be.

CHAPTER 4

THE CHOICE
TO REJOICE!

Everyone wants to be happy. If you ask people what their number one ambition in life is, most people will say, "I just want to be happy." In Orange County, California, where I live, being happy is serious business. I mean, we work at it. It is like no other place in the nation. We have this idea that we must be happy all the time. I must act happy. I must talk happy. I must smell happy. I certainly must look happy. And if I am not happy, I must fake it—put on a mask and remember that I am supposed to be having a great time.

Always having to appear happy creates stress. I see many more people faking happiness than living reality. The fact is, not every day scores a "perfect

10." Not everything always works out according to the way we planned it. Some days are disasters. Let's be honest about it.

It Is a Bad Day When ...

You know it is going to be a bad day when you call your answering service and they tell you it's none of your business. You know it is going to be a bad day when your horn goes off suddenly and remains stuck as you follow a group of Hell's Angels on the freeway. And you know it is going to be a bad day when you sink your teeth into a beautiful steak and they stay there.

It is easy to be happy when everything is going your way. But what about the rest of life? Are you happy only when everything is going your way? If so, you are going to be unhappy for much of your life.

How can we stay positive in a negative world? How can we remain optimistic when everything is falling apart? This is where joy comes in. Galatians 5:22 says, "The fruit of the Spirit is ... joy." And Paul reminds us in Philippians 4:4, "Rejoice in the Lord always. I will say it again: Rejoice!"

Happiness depends on happenings. It comes from the root word *hap*, which means "luck" or "circumstance." "I am happy today because things just happened to turn out right."

Joy is different. It goes deeper. Joy is an attitude, a choice. Joy is an inside job and is not dependent on circumstances. It is your choice to rejoice. That is the basic truth of this chapter: you can choose, regardless of the circumstances, to be joyful.

Joy is what makes life—well—en*joy*able. When we learn to choose joy, we greatly enhance our lives. As Christians we can be the most positive people in the world. Why? Romans 5 gives us three reasons.

We Have Hope

Romans 5 begins with these words: "Therefore, since we have been justified through faith, we have peace with God through our Lord Jesus Christ, through whom we have gained access by faith into this grace in which we now stand" (vv. 1–2). Paul then explains that the result of experiencing the grace of God is that "we rejoice in the hope of the glory of God" (v. 2). For a Christian, no situation is completely hopeless. *Christians have hope.*

It has been said that a person can live forty days without food, three days without water, eight minutes without air, but not one minute without hope. We have to have hope. Some researchers at Cornell University studied 25,000 prisoners of war from World War II. They concluded that a person can handle almost anything if he or she has hope.

Many people have hope, but they have not based it on anything solid. It is an artificial, pump-yourself-up hope. And many people base their hope on the wrong things: the stock market, their good looks, a big salary, a nice job, a good family. But all those things are temporary and can be taken away. When they disappear, so does hope. And joy is impossible without hope.

By contrast, Christians have a reason to be positive. We can rejoice because we rejoice in hope. In Romans 12:12 Paul reminds us, "Be joyful in hope." Paul is talking about our hope in Christ. The hope we have in Christ is the first reason we can rejoice, even in difficult situations.

God Has a Purpose for Our Lives

Second, we can rejoice because *God has a purpose in every situation.* Romans 5:3 says, "We also rejoice in our sufferings, because we know that suffering produces perseverance." The Greek word translated "sufferings" here means "distress," and it refers to anything that puts us under pressure. It is variously translated "trials," "troubles," "pressures," or "problems." Many people have the misconception that when they get rid of their problems, they will be happy. But we are never going to get rid of all our problems as long as we are alive. Don't you find that just when you get rid of a big problem, you notice smaller problems you were unaware of while you were focusing on the big problem? Joy is learning to enjoy life in spite of problems. Joy is not the absence of suffering, but the presence of God. That is why Paul says we rejoice in suffering: God is always with us.

Do not misunderstand this idea of rejoicing in suffering. Paul is not saying you should fake it. He is not talking about being a Pollyanna Christian with a plastic smile on your face, pretending everything is okay, denying reality, and acting as if nothing is wrong. God does not expect you or want you to be a phony or a hypocrite. Paul is not encouraging you to deny that things are bad in your life if they really are. Neither is he talking about masochism. Some Christians have a martyr complex; they think that the more they suffer, the more spiritual they are. "I am really suffering

for Jesus, and therefore I am a great Christian."
Suffering *can* produce good things in your life,
but Paul is not talking about masochism.

Notice that Paul says, "We rejoice *in* our suffering." He is not saying we rejoice *because* of our
suffering. He is not saying we enjoy suffering. He
is saying we rejoice *in* it because we know the suffering has a purpose behind it. Christians can be
positive even in a negative situation because we
know God has a purpose for allowing that problem. We have a perspective that non-Christians do
not have, and our perspective always determines
how we react to the events around us.

Maybe you have heard of the letter a college
student wrote to her parents. It clearly shows how
perspective influences our reactions. The letter
said:

> *Dear Mom and Dad,*
>
> *I'm sorry to be so long in writing. Unfortu-
> nately, all my stationery was destroyed the night our
> dorm was set on fire by the demonstrators. I'm out
> of the hospital now, and the doctors say my eyesight
> should return — sooner or later. The wonderful boy,
> Bill, who rescued me from the fire, kindly offered
> to share his little apartment with me until the
> dorm is rebuilt. He comes from a good family, so*

you won't be surprised when I tell you we're going to be married. In fact, since you've always wanted a grandchild, you'll be glad to know that you'll be grandparents next month.

P.S. Please disregard the above practice in English composition. There was no fire, I haven't been in the hospital, I'm not pregnant, and I don't even have a steady boyfriend. But I did get a D in French and an F in Chemistry, and I just wanted to be sure you received this news in the proper perspective.

Perspective makes all the difference in the world. How you respond to problems at work, problems at home, and health problems depends on your perspective. Paul says that as Christians we can rejoice even in tough times because we have hope and because we know that God is working in our lives. We have perspective.

Paul reminds us, "We know that suffering *produces...*" Suffering can be productive! Problems have a purpose. Your trials and difficulties have value. It is easier to handle suffering when you know there is a purpose in it, that it is not in vain.

I have had the privilege of assisting in the delivery of all three of my children. I have seen the pain on my wife's face during labor, and I now know why they call it "labor." But I have also seen the expression on her face when the nurse lays that brand-new, bundled baby in her weary arms. Her expression reveals that the effort and pain were worth it. They produced a new life!

Now, what exactly does our suffering produce? First, Paul says our suffering produces perseverance (Rom. 5:3). The Greek word for perseverance literally means "the ability to handle pressure." That is what perseverance is—the ability to hang in there when under pressure, to never give up, to keep on keeping on. When we make it through a difficult time without giving up, our character and confidence are strengthened, enabling us to handle even more pressure when it comes in the future.

Paul says next that perseverance produces character (Rom. 5:4). This word occurs only six or seven times in the Bible, and it means "proven reliable." It is like the luggage we talked about that gets bounced around the room. That luggage has character: it is proven reliable. God wants to make you that kind of person, and he uses suffering to do it. He uses the problems in your life to produce perseverance and character. And internal character, not circumstances, produces joy.

Then, Paul says, character produces hope (Rom. 5:4). In the Bible the word *hope* does not mean "I wish" or "I want." It means confidence in Christ's power and confidence in God's promises. Instead of destroying our hope, problems are designed to increase our hope!

No matter whether a problem is brought on by yourself, by other people, or by the devil, God allowed it. If you are a Christian, nothing comes into your life by accident. Grasping the fact that there is a purpose behind our problems is vitally important, but it is also important to understand that problems do not automatically produce perseverance, character, and hope. You may know people who went through tough times, but difficulty and pain did not produce any positive character in their lives. Instead, they became bitter, angry, and uptight. Perseverance, character, and hope are produced in us only when we *choose* the right attitude. And what is the right attitude? *Joy!* When we learn to rejoice in the problem—not *for* but *in* the problem—God uses it for good in our lives.

The book of James echoes Paul's teaching on this subject: "Consider it pure joy, my brothers, whenever you face trials of many kinds, because you know that the testing of your faith develops perseverance" (James 1:2–3). Notice again that joy comes "because you know." It is always a matter of perspective. James continues, "Perseverance must finish its work so that you may be mature and complete, not lacking anything" (v. 4). God says those problems in your life are meant to produce maturity.

No study of Christian joy would be complete without mentioning the book of Philippians. If you really want to understand joy, read Philippians. Nineteen times in this short letter Paul talks about rejoicing and having joy. Mark those verses and meditate on them. Memorize some of them so God can use them to produce joy in your life.

By the way, do you know where Paul was when he wrote this joyful letter? He was in prison! We don't usually think of prison as a place of rejoicing, but Paul had learned to be content in any situation, and his joy did not depend on his circumstances. Christians can be joyful in tough times because they always have hope and because God's purpose is always greater than any problem.

God Is with Us

In Romans 5:11 Paul mentions a third reason we can be joyful: "We rejoice because of what God has done through our Lord Jesus Christ, who has now made us God's friends" (GNT). We can be joyful in any circumstances because God is always with those who believe in him, no matter where we are or what we are facing. As believers we have been reconciled to God through Jesus Christ. We have become God's friends, and this friendship will last forever.

Isaiah 43:2 echoes this assurance:

When you pass through deep waters, I will be with you;
>   your troubles will not overwhelm you.
>   When you pass through fire, you will not be burned;
The hard trials that come will not hurt you (GNT).

You would do well to meditate on and memorize this verse—you may need it this week. It is saying that if you are a believer, God is with you and nothing can overwhelm you. Nothing can destroy you. The devil can't (he doesn't have enough power), other people can't, and God won't. *Nothing can overwhelm you!* No matter what you go through in life, you will never go through it alone. That is reason to rejoice!

DEVELOP A SPIRITUAL WORKOUT

Joy is like a muscle. The more you exercise it, the stronger it becomes. There are four exercises that can help us develop inner joy. Do these four things for the next six weeks and see what a difference they make in your life. They worked in my life years ago when I made the decision to do them. If you do them, I guarantee that you will become a more positive, joyful person than you have ever been.

First, *develop the attitude of gratitude.* First Thessalonians 5:18 says, "Give thanks in all circumstances, for this is God's will for you in Christ Jesus." That is the attitude of gratitude. Notice again that we do not have to be thankful *for* all circumstances; rather, we are to be thankful *in* all circumstances.

Psychologists say that gratitude is the healthiest emotion. Hans Seyle, the father of stress studies, claimed that gratitude produces more emotional energy than any other attitude. Haven't you found it to be true that the people who are the most grateful are the happiest people you know?

I challenge you to look for ways to express gratitude this week and see what a difference it makes. Write a note expressing appreciation to someone, or make a phone call to tell someone how much he or she has meant in your life. And don't forget to express gratitude to God. The psalmist says, "My heart leaps for joy and I will give thanks to him in song" (Ps. 28:7). If you are not a joyful person, start singing hymns of praise to God and watch your attitude change.

Second, *cultivate inner joy by giving*. Jesus teaches us that "it is more blessed to give than to receive" (Acts 20:35). Someone has jokingly said that when it comes to giving, many people will stop at nothing. What does the Bible say? "God loves a cheerful giver" (2 Cor. 9:7). Why? Perhaps it is because we are most like God when we give, and he does not give grudgingly.

In addition, our giving determines how much God can do in our lives. When we give to him gladly, we open ourselves to receive from him freely. Malachi 3:10 says, " 'Bring the whole tithe into the storehouse, that there may be food in my house. Test me in this,' says the LORD Almighty, 'and see if I will not throw open the floodgates of heaven and pour out so much blessing that you will not have room enough for it.'" You have heard of the Pepsi Challenge; this is the Heavenly Challenge! We cannot outgive God. As a godly old farmer once said, "I shovel into God's storehouse, and he shovels into mine—and God has a bigger shovel."

Third, *develop inner joy through service*: give your life to helping others. Jesus said we must lose our life to save it (Mark 8:35). In the book of Ephesians, Paul reminds us, "Serve wholeheartedly, as if you were serving the Lord, not men, because you know that the Lord will reward everyone for whatever good he does" (6:7–8). The happiest people are usually too busy serving others to ask themselves, "Am I happy?"

Joy comes as we get our focus off of ourselves and concentrate on helping others. There are probably several areas of service in your church just waiting for someone like you to fill them. Ask your pastor or Sunday school director if you can do something to help out. It will make their day—after they regain consciousness!

The final exercise aimed at developing inner joy is *sharing Christ with others*. Jesus says there is rejoicing in heaven when a person comes to faith in Christ (Luke 15:10). My greatest joy came when I committed my life to Jesus Christ; my second greatest joy has been to introduce others to him. Imagine the scene in heaven: someone you witnessed to comes over to you and says, "I want to thank you for caring and taking the time. I am here because you cared enough to tell me about Jesus." Now, that will be a time of rejoicing. But that is the culmination of the joy; it begins here and now when you assist in the birth of a new child into the family of God.

Every once in a while I run into a Christian who says, "I've lost my joy." The question I sometimes ask is, "When was the last time you led someone to Christ?" It has usually been a long time. Concerning his fellow Jews, Paul said, "How I wish with all my heart that my own people might be saved! How I pray to God for them!" (Rom. 10:1 GNT) Ask God to give you a burden like that.

Joy is elusive because the very exercises that produce it run counter to what our culture teaches about joy. Our culture says, "Live for yourself and forget about others." But our Lord tells us that joy comes from developing an attitude of gratitude and giving of our material possessions, our time, and our knowledge of the Good News. I challenge you to try these four exercises for six weeks. If you practice them faithfully, you will discover that you have become a more joyful person.

Putting Thoughts into Action

1. What is the difference between joy and happiness, and why is the former preferable to the latter?
2. Why is a more hopeful attitude both valid and effective in dealing with difficult situations?

CHAPTER 5

Peaceful Living
in an Uptight World

Everyone wants peace of mind. Whether we are a businessperson facing the pressures of deadlines at the office, a homemaker trying to corral the kids, or a student just trying to make it through the semester, everyone wants peace of mind. But most of us have to admit that we experience more stress than peace.

How familiar are you with stress? Here is a little quiz. Complete each of these sentences with the appropriate word:

I am ready to throw in the _____.

I am at the end of my _____.

I am just a bundle of _____.

My life is falling _____.

I am at my wits' _____.

I feel like resigning from the human _____.

How did you do? If you answered *towel*, *rope*, *nerves*, *apart*, *end*, and *race* in that order, give yourself an A+. You are an expert on the subject of stress! Most of us have muttered these sayings often enough that they are almost second nature.

Stress is an unfortunate fact of life in our modern world. Everyone is under stress. Everyone is tense. Millions of aspirin are consumed in the United States every day. Sales of tranquilizers are at an all-time high. Books on peace of mind become instant bestsellers.

We are told that too much stress is unhealthy. What else is new? We have known that for centuries. Nearly three thousand years ago, Solomon wrote, "A heart at peace gives life to the body, but envy rots the bones" (Prov. 14:30). The Bible has a lot to say about stress, and even more about its antidote—peace of mind. But what is peace?

You Need Three Kinds of Peace

The Bible talks about three kinds of peace. First is *spiritual peace*. Spiritual peace is peace *with* God. Romans 5:1 says, "Since we have been justified through faith, we have peace with God through our Lord Jesus Christ." That is the foundation, the bottom line. We have to have peace with God before we can have any other kind of peace. I hope you have found that peace. There is only one way to obtain it, and that is through Jesus Christ (John 14:6).

Next comes *emotional peace*. First we must have peace *with* God—spiritual peace. Then we can have the peace *of* God—emotional peace. This is what most of us think about when we think of the word *peace*—an internal sense of well-being and order.

Colossians 3:15 says, "Let the peace of Christ rule in your hearts, since ... you were called to peace." The Greek word translated "rule" here is used only this one time in the Bible, and it means "to umpire." This verse says we should let the peace of God be the umpire in our lives. What does an umpire do? He keeps the peace. He makes sure the game is played in a smooth and orderly manner. God wants to give you an internal umpire who will keep you at peace even when everything around you seems chaotic.

Have you ever heard anyone say, "I need to get away"? Maybe you have said it yourself. Have you ever been so tired at night that your body collapses into the bed but your mind won't turn off? Your mind just races from one thought to another. Well, you *can* get away. You could go to Tahiti today, but if you do not have emotional peace, your mind will still be racing while you are getting a tan on the beach. You cannot run away from yourself. You need both spiritual peace and emotional peace.

Third, you need *relational peace*, or peace with other people. Romans 12:18 says, "If it is possible, as far as it depends on you, live at peace with everyone." Relational peace reduces conflict.

You must know from experience that relationships can be a source of stress. For most of us, our biggest problems are people problems: getting along with the boss, the family, the relatives. We must deal with conflict, competition, and criticism on a regular basis. These things can rob us of peace.

How desperately we need spiritual, emotional, and relational peace! But can we really find it?

UNDERSTAND THE PROMISE OF GOD'S PEACE

In John 14:27 Jesus promised, "I leave behind with you—peace; I give you my own peace and my gift is nothing like the peace of this world. You must not be distressed and you must not be daunted" (Phillips). He spoke these words right before he went to the cross.

Notice that Jesus says his peace is a gift. We cannot work for it, and we cannot earn it. We cannot psych ourselves up for it. We cannot try really hard to get it. It is a gift we simply accept.

Jesus also says that his peace is different from what the world gives. The world's peace is fragile. How many cease-fires have we had in the last few years? Someone has figured out that in the past 3,500 years the world has had just 286 years of peace. The peace of the world is temporary.

Finally, God's peace is not related to circumstances. God's peace allows us to be tranquil in the midst of trouble. So how do we get this peace? There are five keys to acquiring God's perfect peace.

FIVE KEYS TO PERFECT PEACE

Obey God's Principles

First, if we want peace, we must *obey God's principles as found in his Word.* Just do what the Bible says. The psalmist says, "Great peace have they who love your law, and nothing can make them stumble.... I obey your statutes, for I love them greatly" (Ps. 119:165, 167). God says that peace comes when we live in harmony with him—when we do what he tells us to do.

When we buy a new car, there is an owner's manual in the glove compartment. This manual tells us that if we do certain things at certain times, we will get more mileage out of the car.

God's Word is your owner's manual for life. It contains principles for health, finance, marriage, other relationships, business, and much more. You may ignore these principles, but if you do, you have nobody to blame for your problems but yourself. If you do not obey these principles, you will not experience peace. Just as a car runs more smoothly when you operate it according to its design, your life will run more smoothly if you live it according to God's design as presented in his Word. It is that simple. If you want to be at peace, obey God's principles.

Accept God's Pardon

Next, if we want peace, we must *accept God's pardon*, his forgiveness and release from punishment. Guilt is the number one destroyer of peace for most people. When we feel guilty, we feel we are being haunted and chased by our past. What if someone finds out? What if someone sees the skeleton in the closet? That is why we read in newspapers about people who, thirty years after the fact, make restitution for a wrong they committed. They say, "I was living in hell for thirty years and had to get it off my chest." The only way to have peace of mind is to have a clear conscience, and only God can give that.

Micah 7:18 says, "Who is a God like you, who pardons sin and forgives ... transgression? ... You do not stay angry forever but delight to show mercy." Notice that Micah says God is eager—willing and waiting—to clean your slate. It is his nature. He likes to forgive. Someone has said that God has a big eraser. God's Word tells us, "If we confess our sins, he is faithful and just and will forgive us our sins" (1 John 1:9). God's forgiveness is available, so if you do not have a clear conscience, get one today.

Focus on God's Presence

If we want peace, we must *focus on God's presence.* We must realize that God is always with us and learn to sense his presence. Isaiah 26:3 reminds us to fix our gaze on God: "You will keep in perfect peace him whose mind is steadfast, because he trusts in you." We have a choice of focusing on our problems or focusing on God, who holds the solution. Corrie ten Boom, author of *The Hiding Place*, wrote, "The blacker the night around us grew, the brighter and truer and more beautiful burned the Word of God."[1] If you look at the world, you will be distressed; if you look within, you will be depressed; but if you look at Christ, you will be at rest. It is what you concentrate on that determines your level of personal peace. Focus on God's presence; he is with you, and he has promised he will never leave you.

On Friday afternoons in our church office we sometimes do silly things. One Friday afternoon we were playing around with stress dots. Do you know what stress dots are? James Dobson talked about them on his radio program, so we wrote in and got a set. They are little pressure-sensitive dots that you put on your hand. As adrenaline changes in your system, the dots change color and show whether you are under stress. We were experimenting with them to see if we could affect each other's stress level.

I remember saying, "Wouldn't it be great if we had a little internal warning light that told us whenever our focus was off of the Lord? Or if we had a little beep or signal light that told us we were not in tune with God?" Then I realized that we do have a warning light. It is called tension, or stress. Becoming tense is a clear indication that we have taken our eyes off the Lord and placed them on circumstances. We are looking at the problem rather than the solution. When we look at a problem, we are going to get tense. We need to remember that stress is God's way of saying, "Get your focus in order: look at me."

The psalmist says, "God is our refuge and strength, an ever-present help in trouble" (Ps. 46:1). Later in that psalm he reminds us, "Be still, and know that I am God" (v. 10). These verses have an interesting background. They were not written by David; this psalm was written during the time of Hezekiah many years after David lived. The nation of Israel was under attack from Sennacherib, the king of Assyria. Enemy soldiers had surrounded Jerusalem, and the Israelites were uptight. They knew they were going to get whooped, so they prayed this prayer. Five minutes before noon, God smote the Assyrians with a plague, and 185,000 of them died. Jerusalem was saved, and everyone was happy.

This psalm reminds us that God is our refuge. He is our strength no matter how overwhelming the odds seem. He is an ever-present help.

This psalm tells us two things about getting God's help in time of trouble. The first thing is to *be still* when we are in trouble. The Hebrew word here means "to ease up, let go." It has been said that most of our problems come from our inability to sit still. When was the last time you just sat still and focused on the Lord? Try it right now. Take a deep breath, let it out, and focus on God's presence surrounding you.

Do that fifty to sixty times a day, whenever you feel tension building. Take mini-vacations in your mind. Be still. Hurry is the death of prayer.

In addition to telling us to be still, the Lord reminds us, *"Know that I am God."* Did you know that right in the middle of a hurricane or tornado is a quiet center called an eye? Likewise, even though everything is blowing apart around you, there can be a quiet center in your life. Be *still* and *know*. Obey God's principles, accept God's pardon, focus on God's presence, "and the peace of God, which transcends all understanding, will guard your hearts and your minds in Christ Jesus" (Phil. 4:7).

Trust God's Purpose

If we want to experience God's peace, we must *trust God's purpose*. Even when things do not make sense, we must trust God's purpose. Proverbs 3:5–6 says, "Trust in the LORD with all your heart, and lean not on your own understanding; in all your ways acknowledge Him, and He shall direct your paths" (NKJV). There are four verbs in these verses: *trust, lean (not), acknowledge*, and *direct*. The first three verbs are commands. The fourth verb expresses a promise: God will direct your paths.

Let us consider trust. Have you noticed that many things in life do not make sense? And do you feel that a lot of things in life are beyond your control? What do you do in such situations? You trust! That is really all you can do. "Lean not on your own understanding" means "Don't try to figure life out yourself." We do that all the time, don't we? We waste much time and energy always trying to figure things out. God urges us just to trust him.

Most people worry about two common problems: illness and death. We all face the threat of illness, and we all will die someday. How can we have peace when a loved one is terminally ill? How should we respond when a friend dies unexpectedly? God tells us to trust him rather than try to figure things out by ourselves.

People have told me on more than a few occasions that when they finally stopped trying to figure out why God allowed something to happen and just started trusting him, then peace came. We need to face the fact that not all of our questions are going to be answered in this lifetime.

One lesson I am learning slowly is that I don't have to understand *why* or *how* or even *when* God does what he does; all I have to do is trust him in order to experience his peace. As long as I am struggling to figure things out, I am not really trusting God and I probably won't have peace. We have to trust God with our lives and with the lives of our loved ones.

The writer of Proverbs urges us to trust God and not depend on our own understanding. Then he reminds us to acknowledge God—to recognize and accept that God is sovereignly in control of the universe, including the part of the universe you and I inhabit. We must acknowledge that God is in control and that he does not make mistakes.

Someday I am going to preach a sermon on words or phrases we will never hear God say. One of the words is *oops*. God never has to say, "Oops!" because he never makes a mistake. Everything that happens in your life fits into God's plan for you. He uses every situation—even the problems and heartaches and difficulties you bring on yourself—to work out his purpose in your life. He fits everything perfectly into his plan for you. All God expects from you is that you trust him without trying to figure everything out. Acknowledge that God is in control.

When you do this, you have his promise that he will "direct" your life or, as the New International Version puts it, "He will make your paths straight" (Prov. 3:6). Many of us, when we try to direct our own lives, follow haphazard paths filled with indecision: "Should I do this or that? Should I go here or go there?" Indecision produces stress. But when we trust in the Lord, he directs our paths, and he makes them straight, not stressful.

The apostle Paul learned this lesson. He was at peace because he knew God was directing his life. Even when he was locked in a Roman prison, he could write, "I have learned the secret of being content in any and every situation, whether well fed or hungry, whether living in plenty or in want" (Phil. 4:12). Then he tells us the "secret" he has learned: "I can do everything through him who gives me strength" (v. 13). We see that this was something Paul had to *learn*; it didn't come naturally to him any more than it does to us. He *learned* to trust the Lord and to allow him to direct his life—and he was content; he was at peace. The safest, most serene place to be is in the center of God's will.

One of my favorite scenes in the Bible is when Jesus and the disciples are in a fishing boat on the Sea of Galilee and a storm comes up (Luke 8:22–25). What fascinates me is that Jesus could sleep right through that raging storm. From the disciples' reaction, we know the storm was severe. A number of them were experienced fishermen, and had been through many storms. But they did not think they would make it through this one. In the midst of this storm and all the commotion on the boat, Jesus was sound asleep. How could he sleep? Because he knew something the disciples didn't know: God was in control. It didn't look as if he was, but with one word from Jesus, the storm subsided.

Peter learned something from that incident about getting a good night's sleep. Some years later he was arrested by King Herod and put in prison (Acts 12:1–19). The night before Peter was to be executed, God sent an angel to rescue him. Notice that the angel had to strike Peter on the side to wake him up (v. 7). Peter was sleeping like a baby! Why? Because he was trusting the Lord, who was directing his life. That is peace, real peace!

Ask for God's Peace

If we want God's peace, we need to ask for it. In Philippians 4, Paul tells us, "Do not be anxious about anything, but in everything, by prayer and petition, with thanksgiving, present your requests to God. And the *peace of God*, which transcends all understanding, will guard your hearts and your minds in Christ Jesus" (vv. 6–7, emphasis added). Notice the order—first prayer and then peace. There is a cause-and-effect relationship here. Prayer is the cause; peace is the effect.

If you are not praying, you are likely to be worrying. And worry is a useless emotion—such a waste. Worry is the opposite of peace; they cannot coexist. Our word *worry* comes from the German word *wergen*, which means "to choke." That is what worry does—it chokes your life. Jesus indicated this in explaining the parable of the sower in Luke 8: "The seed that fell among thorns stands for those who hear, but as they go on their way they are choked by life's worries, riches and pleasures, and they do not mature" (v. 14).

When pressure builds up, don't panic. Pray! Prayer is a tremendous stress reliever. It can be your safety valve. When pressure builds up and you feel as if you are about to explode, open the safety valve of prayer. Turn your cares into prayers.

I once attended a stress management seminar, and one thing I learned is that everyone needs an unconditional listener to unload on. "Talk to your pet" was one of the suggestions. The principle is a valid one: we need an unconditional listener to unload on, someone who will not become stressed out by our dumping on him or her, someone who will not think any less of us because of what we say. But a heart-to-heart talk with a hamster is not God's ideal. Who better than God to "dump" on? In fact, Peter uses this image when he says, "Cast all your anxiety on him because he cares for you" (1 Peter 5:7). Lay it on the Lord! God will not be stressed out by what you tell him. He already knows everything about you and loves you anyway. The seminar teacher had the right idea; he just didn't know the right person to talk to. Prayer, after all, is talking with God. Tell him what is on your mind, what is troubling you, and acknowledge his control of the universe, including your life. Ask him to meet your needs. He can do that better than a whole herd of hamsters.

"Do not let your hearts be troubled," Jesus told his disciples. "Trust in God; trust also in me" (John 14:1). You will not experience true or lasting peace until Jesus Christ is in charge of your life. Remember: peace is not a trouble-free life; it is a sense of calm in the midst of life's storms.

Conclusion

What is robbing you of peace today? Is it guilt? Turn to God for forgiveness. Is it worry? A job change? Finances? Major surgery? A difficult person? You can talk to Christ about all of these things and anything else that is bothering you. You will feel better for having done so, and perhaps best of all, he can do something about them.

What is your deepest fear? Loneliness? Fear of failure? Death? Illness? Change? Responsibility? Pray this familiar prayer, called the Serenity Prayer:

> *God, grant me the serenity to accept the things*
> *I cannot change, the courage to change the things*
> *I can, and the wisdom to know the difference.*

The wonderful by-product of your prayer will be peace.

PUTTING THOUGHTS INTO ACTION

1. What kind of peace — spiritual, emotional, or relational — are you lacking most right now, and why?
2. Learn the Serenity Prayer by heart and recite it every day.

CHAPTER 6

DEVELOPING
YOUR PATIENCE

The famous psychologist-educator John Dewey said that the most useful virtue in the world is patience. The fact is, we need it all the time, and we need it everywhere. Proverbs 16:32 says, "It is better to be patient than powerful. It is better to win control over yourself than over whole cities" (GNT).

Years ago, while going through a difficult time, I began praying, "Lord, give me more patience." I expected my problems to decrease, but they got worse! Then I said, "Lord, give me more patience," and the problems really got bad! Later I realized that God had indeed answered my prayer. I had become much more patient, thanks to the problems.

By "testing" our patience, God gives us true patience. It is easy to appear patient when everything is going your way. But what happens when things aren't going your way? Perhaps you are like the person who prayed, "Lord, give me patience, and I want it right now!"

A *Peanuts* cartoon begins by showing Lucy praying at her bedside. Then she gets up, walks out, and says to Linus, "I was praying for greater patience and understanding, but I quit." Then in the last frame she says, "I was afraid I might get it."

Test Your Patience

Are you afraid to pray for patience for fear you might get it? How patient are you? Here are four ways to test your patience.

Interruptions

The first test is *interruptions*. We have all experienced these. You sit down to dinner and the phone rings. Or you are in the bathtub and a salesperson comes to the door. Or you are working on a deadline and visitors arrive. Our best plans are often interrupted.

Do you have to deal with interruptions at work? Take heart! When Johannes Brahms was writing his "Lullaby," he had so many interruptions of consequence that it took him seven years to compose the piece. Yes, the problem was interruptions, although some people think he just kept falling asleep at the piano.

Jesus' disciples disliked interruptions. They became impatient with people who interrupted Jesus' schedule (Matt. 19:13–14). They said, "Don't bring your kids to Jesus now. The Master is busy."

How do you handle interruptions? That is the first test of your patience.

Inconveniences

Inconveniences are the second test of your patience. How do you deal with inconveniences in your life? Americans hate to be delayed. We are the "Now Generation." We have a microwave mentality—we want what we want in seconds. We have Minute Rice, instant coffee, and fast food. We don't like to wait.

We also want our information on the spot; we like up-to-date reports. At election time, pollsters report election results before many people have even voted. A hundred years ago people didn't worry if they missed a stagecoach; they could always catch another one in a day or two. Today we have a heart attack if we miss a revolving door! We are in such a hurry. We have to get going. We can't wait!

Luke 10:40 tells us about a woman who had trouble being patient in the face of inconvenience. Jesus was at the home of Mary and Martha, and Martha was busily preparing the meal. Martha was upset with her sister because Mary had left her to do all the work. You can hear the edge in her voice as she said to Jesus, "Lord, don't you care that my sister has left me to do the work by myself? Tell her to help me!" Maybe you feel this way. Maybe you are carrying that extra load and you feel put upon and inconvenienced. You would like to be sitting at Jesus' feet too, but there is work to be done and you are the only one who seems to be aware of it. How do you react? Are you patient despite the inconvenience?

Irritations

The third test of your patience is *irritations*—those little things in life that bug you. Here is a list of some irritations I have heard about in the last month: traffic jams, long lines, phone calls, misplaced keys, cold food, late planes, flat tires, occupied bathrooms, neighborhood rock groups. You could make your own list, I'm sure. Some of these irritations are controllable, but most of them aren't. So we have to learn to cope. How do you handle them? It takes patience.

As we read in Numbers 20:10–11, Moses became irritated with the Israelites on one particular occasion. He had put up with their petty complaints and criticisms for years, and now he had no patience left. When God told him to speak to the rock to get water, he struck it in anger instead. His impatience caused him to disobey God. As a result, God did not allow him to enter the Promised Land. Moses was usually a patient person, but even patient people have their limits, or so it would seem.

The *Encyclopaedia Britannica 1982 Yearbook*, under the heading "Strange and Unusual Events," tells about a man named Brian Heise:

> Brian Heise had more than his share of luck in July, and most of it was bad. When his apartment in Provo, Utah, became flooded from a broken pipe in the upstairs apartment, the manager told him to go out and rent a water

vacuum. That's when he discovered his car had a flat tire. He changed it, then went inside again to phone a friend for help. The electric shock he got from the phone so startled him that he inadvertently ripped the instrument off the wall. Before he could leave the apartment a second time, a neighbor had to kick down the apartment door because water damage had jammed it tight. While all of this was going on, someone stole Heise's car, but it was almost out of gas. He found it a few blocks away but had to push it to the gas station, where he filled up the tank. That evening Heise attended a military ceremony at Brigham Young University. He injured himself severely when he somehow sat on his bayonet, which had been tossed onto the front seat of his car. Doctors were able to stitch up the wound, but no one was able to resuscitate four of Heise's canaries that were crushed to death by falling plaster. After Heise slipped on the wet carpet and badly injured his tailbone, he said he began to wonder if "God wanted me dead, but just kept missing."[1]

And you think you've had bad days!

For many of us, our greatest irritations in life are people. Perhaps you feel like the taxi driver in

New York who said, "You know, it's not just the work that I enjoy, but it's the people I run into."

We all run into people who are irritating or get us down somehow. We must learn the lessons of the oyster. The oyster takes an irritation—a grain of sand—and turns it into a pearl. Learning to respond to irritations positively will enable you to transform your irritations into pearls.

Inactivity

The fourth test of your patience is *inactivity*. Most of us would rather do anything but wait. We hate to wait in the doctor's office, stand in line at the supermarket, or be confined to bed rest.

Did you know that you will spend six months of your life sitting at red lights waiting for them to turn green? And have you noticed that when the light turns green, if you don't move in two seconds, the guy behind you turns red? Isn't it interesting how we admire patience in the driver who is behind us but not in the one ahead of us? How do you handle inactivity?

You can learn a lot about people by watching how they wait for an elevator to come to their floor. Some people are swayers; they kind of sway back and forth. Some people are bouncers; they bounce up and down while waiting for the elevator to begin moving. Some people are pushers; they repeatedly push the button, as if that were going to make the elevator come any faster. They just can't stand and wait. They have to do something to feel they are in control.

We often speak of "the patience of Job." Job is an example of a man who could do nothing but wait. He said, "All the days of my hard service I will wait for my renewal to come" (Job 14:14). We can learn much from Job's example.

The Bible says, "Impatience will get you into trouble" (Prov. 19:2 GNT). Medical researchers agree with that. They have discovered a whole new disease called "hurry sickness." Drs. Meyer Friedman and Ray H. Rosenman say that 90 percent of heart attack victims have this "hurried" type A personality.[2] Their habitual impatience gets them into trouble.

How to Become a Patient Person

What causes impatience? A lack of peace. Perhaps that is why God put *patience* right after *peace* in the list of the fruit of the Spirit. When you have peace in your heart, almost nothing can make you impatient. But when you do not have peace in your

106

heart, almost anything can make you impatient. So how can you learn to be a patient person? The Bible reveals a four-part answer.

Develop a New Perspective

First, *develop a new perspective*. Find a new way of looking at the situation or the person that is giving you problems. Patience begins by changing the way you view something. When I am impatient, I have a limited perspective. All I see is myself: *my* needs, *my* desires, *my* goals, *my* wants, *my* schedule, and how people are messing up *my* life. The root of impatience is selfishness. So I need to get a new perspective on life. I need to learn to see things from other people's points of view.

Would you like to know the secret of success? If you want to be a successful husband or wife, learn to see life from your partner's point of view. If you want to be a successful parent, learn to see life from your child's point of view. If you want to be a successful businessperson, learn to see life from your customers' point of view. If you want to be a successful employer, learn to see life from your employees' point of view. Look at the situation from the other's perspective and discover why that person feels as he or she does. I don't know of anything that has greater potential for reducing conflict in your life.

Now look at what the writer of the book of Proverbs says: "A man's wisdom gives him patience; it is to his glory to overlook an offense" (Prov. 19:11). Notice the word *wisdom*. What is wisdom? Wisdom is seeing life from God's point of view, getting God's perspective on a situation. From that perspective I gain three important insights. (1) I am only human; I am not God. Of course, God knows that, but he wants me to acknowledge it also. I am not perfect, and I am not in control. In fact, most of the things I face in life I cannot control. (2) No one else is perfect either, so I should not be surprised or overly upset when people make mistakes or let me down. (3) God is in control, and he can use the situations, the irritations, and the problems that come into my life to accomplish his purposes for me.

Another verse in Proverbs declares, "A man's steps are directed by the LORD" (20:24). This means you may experience some divine delays, some heavenly interruptions. Sometimes God will put irritating people around you for the purpose of teaching you something. Get a new perspective. Look at it from God's point of view. All through the Bible, God equates patience with maturity. Proverbs 14:29 tells us, "A patient man has great understanding, but a quick-tempered man displays folly." Patience is a mark of maturity. Most children are very impatient; they don't know the difference between "no" and "not yet." When babies don't get what they want immediately, they get very upset. Maturity involves the ability to wait, to live with delayed gratification. A person of understanding and wisdom, who sees life from God's point of view, can be patient. So we need to discover a new perspective.

Acquire a Sense of Humor

A second way to become a patient person is to *develop a sense of humor.* Learn to laugh at your circumstances. Learn to laugh at yourself. Somehow find the fun in the frustrating. Proverbs 14:30 says, "A relaxed attitude lengthens a man's life" (LB).

Scientific studies show that people who laugh live longer. Humor is a tension dissolver. It is an antidote to anxiety. It is a tranquilizer without any troublesome side effects. Laughter is life's shock absorber. Someone once asked President Lincoln how he handled the stresses of the Civil

War. He said, "If it hadn't been for laughter, I could not have made it." Many famous comedians grew up in poor neighborhoods with lots of problems. They coped with their troubles by learning to laugh and making others laugh.

So learn to laugh. If you can laugh at it, you can live with it. And besides, if you learn to laugh at your troubles, you will never run out of anything to laugh at!

God has a sense of humor. Have you ever seen the face of an orangutan? God thought that one up! Do you want to be more like God? Learn to laugh. A sense of humor can preserve your sanity.

God's timing is as marvelous as his sense of humor. As I was typing the notes for this chapter, I somehow completely lost my outline. So I said to myself, "Self, you have a choice here. You can either practice what you preach and laugh this situation away, or you can get upset and irritated." I am sure my wife and my kids were wondering what I was laughing about. Learn to laugh. It's relaxing.

Life is full of funny situations. Will Rogers once said, "I don't know any jokes. I just watch the government and report the facts." Proverbs 17:22

says, "Being cheerful keeps you healthy" (GNT). We all need to develop a sense of humor.

Deepen Your Love

The third step in becoming a patient person is to *deepen your love*. First Corinthians 13:4 is probably one of the most straightforward verses in the Bible: "Love is patient." This means that when I am impatient, I am being unloving, because love is patient. When you love someone, you care about that person's needs, desires, hurts, and point of view—not just your own. When you are filled with love, almost nothing can provoke you to anger or cause you to be impatient. When you are filled with anger, almost anything can provoke you. When you are under pressure, whatever is inside is going to come out. So deepen your love.

Ephesians 4:2 says, "Be patient with each other, making allowance for each other's faults because of your love" (LB). Why should you be patient with others? "Because of your love."

When I was in college, one fellow bugged me a lot. To make matters worse, he went out of his way to be around me. He was one of those people who spits on you when he talks. The situation became so bad that when he would walk down the hallway, I would turn around and leave the building just to avoid him. I really did not like this guy; he was an irritation to me.

Then one night I read Ephesians 4:2, and it was like a dagger in my heart. "God, I don't love that guy," I confessed. Do you recall that earlier in this book I said that you do not have to like certain people but you do have to love them? Love is not a feeling; it's a choice. And an action. So that night at college I said, "God, help me love this person tomorrow. Not forever. Just help me to love him tomorrow." And then I prayed a prayer I later regretted. I said, "God, if this guy's irritating me is going to make me more like Christ, then make me like Christ. Teach me patience. If this guy's bugging me is going to make me more like you, I pray that tomorrow he will irritate me more than I have ever been irritated before in my life." That was a mistake.

I got up the next morning and went to classes, but I did not see this person the whole day. I thought, *Hey, this is great! I love this way of learning patience. Right on, Lord!* Then dinnertime came. I walked into the cafeteria, got my meal, and sat down. As I was eating my dinner, this guy spied me, sauntered over, and said, "Hey,

Rick, I haven't seen you all day!" He slammed his tray down. His spaghetti covered my head and my shirt, and his Coke spilled all over my pants. Everybody in the cafeteria turned to look at me, spaghetti dripping down from my ears. But at that point I was filled with love and peace and joy because I was prepared. I really was—I had been praying all day. So I simply said, "Praise the Lord!" I'm sure everyone thought I had gone off my rocker.

What happens when you praise God for people who irritate you? You may become so much more like Jesus that they won't bother you anymore. Or if it is the devil using that person to get at you, he will stop because the situation is motivating you to praise God. If you learn to praise God in every situation, you will develop a wall of praise around your life that even the devil cannot penetrate.

Depend on the Lord

The final step in developing patience is to *depend on God*. Patience is not merely a matter of human willpower; it is the fruit of the Spirit. You cannot just psych yourself up and say, "I'm going to be patient if it kills me." It will. Patience is not willpower. Patience is not saying, "He doesn't really irritate me," when deep inside you are really thinking, *I hate that guy.* Patience is not wearing a mask and pretending.

If it is God's patience you feel, if it is the genuine fruit of the Spirit, you will have a genuine inner peace. Certain situations won't bother you the way they used to. Why? Because you are depending on the Lord.

Patience is a form of faith. It says, "I trust God. I believe that God is bigger than this problem. And I believe that God has his hand in these irritations and can use them in my life for good." Faith helps us look at life from God's point of view. Faith helps us say, "God, what do you want me to learn in this situation?" instead of "Why did this happen?" Because of faith we no longer need to ask God, "Why did I get a flat tire while I was on the way to an important appointment?" Instead, we can ask, "What do you want me to learn from this predicament?"

Noah had to wait 120 years before the promised rain came. That is a long time to be patient. Abraham waited a hundred years to have a son. That is a long time to be patient. Moses waited forty years in the desert and then spent another forty years leading the children of Israel across the desert to the Promised Land. That is a long time to be patient. Everyone in Old Testament times was waiting for the Messiah to come. In New Testament days, the disciples waited in the upper room for the Holy Spirit. The Bible is a book about waiting. Why? Because waiting demonstrates faith, and faith pleases God.

The hardest kind of waiting happens when you are in a hurry and God is not. It is hard to be patient when you are waiting for an answer to prayer; waiting for a miracle to happen; or waiting for God to change your financial condition or your health problem or your children, wife, husband, or that relative who is a kook. It is hard when you are in a hurry and God isn't, but waiting patiently is an evidence of faith. It is also a test of faith. How long can you wait?

Lazarus was a good friend of Jesus who became very sick. Mary and Martha, his sisters, sent word to Jesus, saying, "Lord, the one you love is sick" (John 11:3). The Bible says that when Jesus heard this, he purposely waited two more days before he set out for Bethany, the town where they lived. By the time he arrived, Lazarus had died. His body was already sealed in the tomb.

From all appearances, Jesus arrived too late. Yet Jesus knew it was not too late. He walked up to the tomb and called, "Lazarus, come out!" (John 11:43). And Lazarus did come out—alive!

The point is that God is never late; his timing is perfect. He may not move according to our schedule (he usually doesn't), but he is always on time. He wants us to trust him and wait on him. The psalmist puts it this way: "Be still before the LORD and wait patiently for him" (Ps. 37:7). Earlier in this psalm the writer instructs us to "trust" in the Lord, to "delight" in him, and to "commit" our way to him (vv. 3–5). These are all aspects of faith and dependence. God longs for us to trust him more than anything else. Patience is evidence of our faith in him.

Why should we be patient? Because God is patient, and we are to be like him. Peter urges us, "Bear in mind that our Lord's patience means salvation" (2 Peter 3:15). God is patient. If we are his children, we should bear the family likeness. That is why the Holy Spirit is at work in our lives producing patience in us. It is a part of the character of Christ.

Putting Thoughts into Action

1. Which test of patience—interruption, inconvenience, irritation, inactivity—is affecting you the most at this time?
2. Think of one person with whom you are angry and impatient. What steps will you take to change those feelings?

CHAPTER 7

PUTTING ON
A LITTLE KINDNESS

In our study on the fruit of the Spirit, we have looked at love, joy, peace, and patience. Now we come to the fruit of kindness. Colossians 3:12 says, "Therefore, as God's chosen people, holy and dearly loved, clothe yourselves with compassion, kindness, humility, gentleness and patience." Notice the word *clothe*. The Greek word literally means "put on." What Paul is saying here is that when we wake up in the morning, we ought to get dressed spiritually and emotionally as well as physically. When we wake up in the morning and decide what to wear, we should also ask ourselves, "What kind of attitude am I going to wear today?"

Paul says kindness is a choice. It is something we can choose to "put on" every day.

Kindness is "love in action"—a practical expression of love. It is visible and active, not just emotional. There is a song that says, "Find the need and fill it. Find the hurt and heal it." That is kindness.

But why should we be kind? After all, kindness can be risky. We might be misunderstood if we are kind to others. They might think, "Why is this person being so nice? What's in it for him?" People we are kind to also might take advantage of us. They might become parasites with the attitude, "Oh, here's a sucker. I'll milk him for all he's worth."

Despite the risks, we are to be kind for two reasons. First, we are to be kind because God is kind to us. Ephesians 2:8 says, "Because of his kindness you have been saved through trusting Christ" (LB). Grace and kindness always go together. Poet Robert Burns said that the kind heart most resembles God. We should be kind just because God is kind to us.

The other reason we should be kind is that we want people to be kind to us. We want to be treated right. Jesus said, "Do to others what you would have them do to you" (Matt. 7:12). If you are rude to other people, they are going to be rude to you. But if you are kind, most people will want to respond the same way. Proverbs 21:21 says, "Be kind and honest and you will live a long life; others will respect you and treat you fairly" (GNT). In Proverbs 11:17 we read, "Your own soul is nourished when you are kind; it is destroyed when you are cruel" (LB). So when we are kind, we are really doing ourselves a favor.

What does it mean to be a kind person, and how can we become kinder? Let me suggest five characteristics of a kind person.

Be Sensitive

First, kind people are *sensitive* to others. They are aware of the needs of people around them. So become aware of the needs of those around you. Tune in to them. Kindness always starts with sensitivity. Philippians 2:4 says, "Each of you should look not only to your own interests, but also to the interests of others." Circle the word *look*. Kindness always starts with noticing the needs and hurts of others.

Often in marriage we are totally unaware of what our partner's needs are. We have become calloused. We have stopped listening. We are oblivious to the pressure our mate is under. Simply stated, the root of many marriage problems is insensitivity.

Everyone you meet this week needs kindness because everyone is hurting somewhere. Even the people who sit around you at church have major hurts. It's just that you are not aware of them most of the time. So kindness starts with sensitivity.

We find an example of sensitivity and kindness in the life of King David as recorded in 2 Samuel 9. David was crowned king of Israel and had led the Israelites in a series of military victories. The former King Saul, who had opposed him and chased him for years, was dead. David's friend, Jonathan—Saul's son—had been killed. Now, safely enthroned for several years, David made an unusual request. He asked whether there was anyone left in Saul's family to whom he could be kind. He found Saul's grandson—Jonathan's son—Mephibosheth, who was crippled in both feet.

When David sent for him, Mephibosheth probably thought, *I am going to be killed because I am part of the enemy family, the old dynasty.* But notice David's kind words: "Don't be afraid,... for I will surely show you kindness for the sake of your father Jonathan. I will restore to you all the land that belonged to your grandfather Saul, and you will always eat at my table" (2 Sam. 9:7). Mephibosheth's response is interesting: "What is your servant, that you should notice a dead dog like me?" (v. 8). He apparently had a poor self-image. But the point is that David actively looked for people to whom he could be kind. He was sensitive. How about you? To whom do you need to be kind this week? To whom do you need to be sensitive?

Be Supportive

A second characteristic exhibited by kind people is *supportiveness*. This means talking about building people up rather than tearing them down. Watch what you say to people. Be supportive in your speech. Speak kindly. Proverbs 15:4 says, "Kind words bring life, but cruel words crush your spirit" (GNT). Nobody likes to be put down. Children say, "Sticks and stones may break my bones, but names will never hurt me." Baloney! Names do hurt! Labels hurt! In fact, the Bible says that death and life are in the power of the tongue. You can destroy others with what you say to them. So build people up with your words. Give everyone you meet an emotional lift. Encourage them. Be supportive.

Proverbs 10:32 says, "Righteous people know the kind thing to say, but the wicked are always saying things that hurt" (GNT). Are you the kind of person who will pounce on a weakness in someone else? Maybe you do it in a joking manner, but you do it, and you enjoy doing it. By contrast, kind people do not embarrass others.

I saw a cartoon in which Charlie Brown is talking on the phone to a girl who says, "Hey, Chuck, guess what I'm running for? The Queen of the May at our school."

Charlie Brown says, "That's very interesting. Lucy has always been chosen at our school."

The girl on the phone responds, "Your school has pretty low standards, huh, Chuck?"

After Charlie Brown hangs up the phone, he looks at Lucy and says, "She says, 'Congratulations.'" Now that's diplomacy. That's kindness.

How supportive are you in speaking to others? Do you encourage or discourage with your words? Do you lift up or tear down? Do you brag on your kids, or do you nag them? Let's put it this way—if God gave you a dollar for every kind word you said and took away a dollar for every unkind word you said, would you be rich or poor? Learn to be sensitive. Be supportive in your speech.

Joseph is a good example of a man who spoke kind words. Everything seemed to go wrong in Joseph's life. His brothers treated him like dirt. In fact, they put him in a pit and sold him into slavery. Everything seemed to go wrong during the first thirty years of his life: he was falsely accused of adultery, he was put into prison, he was the victim of broken promises. But later the tables were turned, and Joseph became second in command in all of Egypt. His brothers came to him on bended knee, and at that time Joseph had the opportunity to retaliate and get even. But the Bible says that Joseph reassured them and spoke kindly to them, even after their father — the person Joseph would most want to please — had died (Gen. 50:19 – 21). Kind words can build a bridge in a strained relationship. A Christian ought to speak kindly even when given the opportunity to retaliate.

BE SYMPATHETIC

A third characteristic of a kind person is the ability to be *sympathetic*. If you want to be kind, learn to be sympathetic. People appreciate it when you sympathize with them, when you grieve with them and hurt with them. Many times when someone is experiencing a crisis, other people say, "We feel so awkward. We just don't know what to say at times like this." Actually, you don't have to *say* anything. Just being there is an expression of kindness. Sometimes a touch on the shoulder, a tear, a pat on the back, or a grasp of the hand is all a hurting person needs. That is kindness. Romans 12:15 says, "When others are happy, be happy with them. If they are sad, share their sorrow" (LB).

Regardless of what they think of his politics, most people admit that former President Reagan knew how to express heartfelt emotion. When the space shuttle exploded or when a plane carrying American soldiers crashed, he greeted the victims' families with a hug, a grasp of the hand, a tear in his eye. Strong leaders are not afraid to show emotion. Weak leaders, on the other hand, worry about what other people think. Strong leaders are strong enough to be sympathetic.

In 2 Timothy 2:24, Paul says that kindness is a mark of spiritual leadership. This means, husbands, that if you are not kind to your wife and children, you are not much of a spiritual leader, no matter how powerful or spiritual you appear in public. How long has it been since you helped with the dishes? How long has it been since you changed a diaper or helped pick up around the house? You say, "I'm the spiritual leader; I don't do that kind of thing." The Bible says kindness is a mark of a spiritual leader.

How do you respond when your teenager comes home with a broken heart? Do you say, "Oh, that's no big deal"? Or do you sympathize? Do you remember *your* teenage years—those years of self-conscious embarrassment? Do you remember when you got a pimple and you felt as if it were a national crisis? But now when your teenager mopes over a newly acquired zit, you say, "Oh, it's no big deal." Of course it is no big deal to you now, but remember that it was a big deal to you when you were a teenager, and it is a big deal to your teenager now. So sympathize with him or her.

Do you get excited about the things your kids get excited about? That is not childish; it's kindness. Get excited with those who are excited. Some people have to have a bomb explode under them before they will get excited about anything. But as the Bible says, "Rejoice with those who rejoice, weep with those who weep" (Rom. 12:15 NRSV).

Now, the supreme example of a sympathetic person is Jesus. As we saw in chapter 6, Jesus wept at the tomb of Lazarus. Jesus was not afraid to show emotion. He is called "the kindness and love of God" (Titus 3:4). Jesus is the embodiment of kindness. We often read in the Gospels that Jesus was "moved with compassion." If you want to know what kindness is like, just look at Jesus.

You must be kind if you want to be like Christ. No matter how many Bible verses you have memorized or how often you go to church, if you are not kind, you are not like Jesus. So learn to be a kind person by being sensitive, supportive, and sympathetic.

Be Straightforward

A kind person is also *straightforward*. Sometimes kindness means being candid. Sometimes it means laying it on the line, telling the truth, leveling with people. Sometimes the kindest thing you can do is to be frank with a friend and tell that person exactly where he or she is wrong. Proverbs 27:6 says, "Wounds from a friend are better than kisses from an enemy!" (LB). A real friend will level with you and say such things as, "You're blowing it" or "You need to get in shape" or "You're making the biggest mistake of your life."

Suppose a doctor examines you, finds something seriously wrong, and then says either "You must have surgery" or "Relax and don't worry about it." Which is the kinder statement? If you need surgery, the kind thing is for the doctor to tell you that you need it. Like a surgeon who takes his knife and cuts open a patient, we sometimes have to hurt people in order to help them heal. Sometimes kindness means being straightforward.

We tend to sugarcoat kindness. The word *kindness* brings to mind a picture of a little, white-haired old lady baking a pie for her neighbor. We don't realize that sometimes kindness means telling painful truth. James Dobson has written a great book about marriage and family relationships entitled *Love Must Be Tough*. Dobson explains that love sometimes means doing the tough thing, saying, "I'm not going to let you get away with this. I'm not going to sit by in silence and let you ruin our marriage."[1] Sometimes I want to ask couples in counseling when they are going to care enough to get mad and say, "I want our marriage to work, and I'm not going to put up with this mess!" Loving husbands and wives care enough to confront each other. Likewise, out of kindness, parents sometimes have to confront their children and say no.

A biblical example of this kind of confrontation is found in Galatians 2. Peter was visiting the church at Antioch, which was made up largely of Gentile Christians, and he was enjoying their fellowship. Peter had learned that as a Christian he didn't have to follow all the old Jewish customs. I think Peter probably developed a good taste for ham sandwiches: "Hey, these are good! I've been missing out all these years." When the Antioch Christians had picnics, Peter probably ate his ham sandwich and visited with his Gentile friends.

One day some Jewish Christians came down from Jerusalem to Antioch, and Peter said, "Maybe I had just better sit over here and pretend I'm not liberated." When Paul saw this, he said, "Peter, you are being a hypocrite." He said this because he cared. Paul cared both for Peter and for the Gentile Christians, who were getting mixed messages. Paul cared enough to confront. Sometimes the kindest thing you can do is say, "You are messing up your life."

How do you know when to be confrontational? How do you know when to be tough rather than tender with people? Ask yourself two questions: First, am I really committed to this person's best interest? Second, am I making a "hit-and-run" comment, or do I plan to stick around and help my friend work out the change? Sometimes kindness means being straightforward—caring enough to confront—and saying, "I am not going to let you destroy yourself. I am not going to sit quietly and watch you mess up your life."

Be Spontaneous

Finally, if you want to be kind, learn to be *spontaneous*. Do not wait to show a kindness. Do it while you have the opportunity. Do it now. Be spontaneous.

Galatians 6:10 says, "As we have opportunity, let us do good to all people, especially to those who belong to the family of believers." Note the phrase "as we have opportunity." When should we be kind? Whenever we have the opportunity.

On some occasion you probably have thought, *That person was really nice to me. I ought to write him a little thank-you note.* Or maybe you have thought, *I need to make that phone call* or *I need to send a little gift* or *I want to take something over to the neighbors.* Then you may have delayed doing the kind deed. And you kept delaying until you were so embarrassed that you didn't do it. I suppose we all have had similar experiences. Yet, when it comes to kindness, good intentions don't count. The opportunity may not last until you "get around to it." Scripture says that when you have the opportunity to be kind, you need to be spontaneous and do it.

When you get the slightest inclination to call your mother, do it. Write a note, share a prayer request, babysit, help around the house, wash the car, mow the lawn, whatever—just be kind whenever you have the opportunity.

The classic example of spontaneous kindness in Scripture is the Good Samaritan. A man was beaten by robbers and left naked and half dead on the side of the road. A priest came along, looked at him, and said, "Oh, I don't want to be near that guy. I would be defiled." Another religious leader came along later and walked right on past. Then a Samaritan came by—a person considered by the Jews to be of an inferior race. The Samaritan bound up the man's wounds, took him to the nearest Holiday Inn, and left his American

Express card with the innkeeper, saying, "Take care of him and charge it to my account. I'll stop by on my way back."

Kindness costs, but when the Samaritan saw the need, he didn't think twice. He dropped everything without hesitation. He was spontaneous. Contrast the Samaritan to the cold, calculating priest and the religious leader, who were trying to figure out if their contributions would be tax deductible. The priest probably had plenty of excuses besides the strict rules that in themselves would have kept him from helping the man in need. Perhaps he thought, *Hey, I did my duty at the temple. I'm in a hurry to get home.* He might have thought, *If I stop and help that guy, I might get robbed myself. I have to think of my family.* Maybe he thought, *It's not my fault he got hurt. He should have been more careful.* Or maybe he vowed to himself, *I will campaign for better police protection on the road to Jericho.*

Here is the point: Jesus told this story to remind us of all the people around us who are hurting. They are hurting in their marriages. They are hurting at work. They are hurting physically, emotionally, and spiritually. The questions I must ask myself are, What is my excuse for not helping them? and Why am I not a kind person?

If you don't remember anything else in this chapter, get this: *The number one enemy of kindness is busyness.* How often we say, "I am just too busy. I don't have time to get involved. It might mess up my schedule. I have my priorities and pressures to think about. I am too busy to fix a meal for my sick neighbor. I am too busy to help with the preschoolers in Sunday school. I am too busy. I don't have time." If that's your response, then you really are too busy, because the ministry of kindness is for everyone.

Be Kind to Someone This Week

It is one thing to read in a book about becoming a kind person, but it is another thing to consider how you are going to be kind this week. Take a few minutes to answer this question: In what specific way can I be kinder this week? Kindness starts with sensitivity, so be aware. Open your eyes and look around you.

Your world is filled with people who need your kindness. How can you be kind at home? I have seen many struggling marriages that could be saved if people would just be kind to each other and treat each other with simple respect. One wife said, "The only time my husband talks to me is when he wants sex or wants me to hand him the remote control." How can you be kind at home? You can start with common courtesy. Sometimes we are rudest to those closest to us. How about your kids? Are you kind to them? Do you pay close attention to them, or do you just herd them here and there like cattle?

What about your crabby boss? You may not like the guy, but you can still be kind to him. How about the new coworker who is floundering at work because no one has given her an orientation? And how about that person who was unkind to you? Unkind people need massive doses of kindness.

Who can you be kind to at church? When you see a stranger, you can smile. You can sit next to a visitor. Welcome him. Shake his hand. Offer to give directions to a Sunday school class. When church members are kind, they speak encouraging words to one another. They smile at people they don't know. Only a locked door could keep people out of a friendly church.

There are as many ways to show kindness as there are people who need it. Let me suggest a project for you this week. Make a list of seven people to whom you can be kind. Also write down *how* you can show kindness to each one this week. Then ask God to give you the opportunity to show kindness to at least one of these people each day. You may be surprised how good this will make you feel. And you will probably find yourself exceeding your quota.

It is an interesting fact of history that the Romans confused the Greek word *christos* (Christ) with the word *chrestos*, which means "kind." See how many people you can *confuse* this week.

PUTTING THOUGHTS INTO ACTION

1. Describe a situation when being straightforward in the right way helped a relationship with someone important to you.
2. In what specific way will you show kindness to someone this week?

CHAPTER 8

LIVING THE
GOOD LIFE

How would you define the word *good*? It is a word we use a lot. We talk about good food, good weather, and a good report. We say, "Have a good day" or "He did a good job" or "It's a good distance from here." The word is used in many different ways.

When I was a teenager, my parents used to say, "Now have fun and be good." Your parents probably said that to you too. I always thought the statement was a contradiction: how could I have fun and be good at the same time?

I looked up the word *good* in Webster's dictionary and found seventeen different categories for the word with three or four different uses or illustrations under each category. Likewise, the Greek and Hebrew words for "good" and "goodness" used in the Bible are varied and full of meaning. The Bible has much to say about goodness. In fact, the words *good* and *goodness* are used 619 times in the Bible.

One phrase we hear often is "the good life." In my part of the country I hear, "Live the good life in Southern California!" But what is the good life?

What Is the Good Life?

For some people the good life means *looking good*. In America, looking good is serious business. Tanning, color coordination, expensive hairdos, fat suction—whatever it takes—we have to look good. We place a high premium on beauty and good looks. Do you know the problem with looking good? There is no universal standard. What looks good to you may not look good to me and vice versa. Have you ever argued with your kids about what clothes they should wear? Looking good means different things to different people.

Some people think the good life means *feeling good*. Whatever it takes, they have to feel good. That may mean sitting in a hot tub, going to

Disneyland, or taking drugs. They pursue pleasure at all costs. Their standard of living is "If it feels good, do it."

Still other people think the good life means *having goods*. They set about acquiring things, and if they get all the goodies, they think they have a good life. They live the bumper sticker slogan "The one with the most toys wins." For these people, the whole object of life is to make money and spend it on goods.

The Bible presents a radically different picture of the good life. God says in his Word that the good life is not based on looking good, feeling good, or having goods. He says the good life is a life filled with goodness — being and doing good. When you are *being* good and *doing* good, you are going to feel good, and you are even going to start looking good — or at least looking better. But what *exactly* is goodness?

Genesis 1 records God's creating of the universe and tells us that when he saw everything he created, he said it was good. Why? Because it fulfilled the purpose for which it was created. "Goodness" means fulfilling a purpose. It is being what God meant you to be.

God made you for a purpose. When you live the way God intends for you to live, you will feel good. Your life will become meaningful. You will feel good because you are doing what God made you to do. Now, what is that good thing for which God made you?

Ephesians 2:10 says, "For we are God's workmanship, *created* in Christ Jesus *to do good works*, which God prepared in advance for us to do" (emphasis added). We are not saved *by* good works; we are saved *for* good works. The Christian lifestyle is to be a lifestyle of goodness. That is the main truth I want you to grasp from this chapter.

But why should you be good? How will you benefit from a lifestyle of goodness? The payoff is a healthy self-esteem. When you are doing good and being good, you will feel good about yourself because you are doing what God created you to do. This is a deeper sense of satisfaction than the satisfaction of self-centered pleasure-seekers. Lasting, healthy self-esteem does not come from looking good, because looks fade. It does not come from feeling good, because you won't feel good all the time, no matter what you do. And it does not come from having goods, because material possessions are often here today and gone tomorrow. Lasting self-esteem comes from doing good and being good. That is the purpose for which God made you.

We Are Not Naturally Good

But there is a problem: *it is not our nature to be good*. We were all born with a natural inclination toward selfishness. As I was flipping the channels on the TV one day, I heard a man saying, "My religion is the belief in the complete, inherent goodness of man." When I heard that, I started laughing. Where had he been living for the past half century—the North Pole? I don't buy the idea of man's inherent goodness at all. It doesn't make sense for four reasons.

First, the Bible says the inherent good of humankind is a fallacy. Isaiah 53:6 tells us that all people want to do their own thing, walk their own way, and be their own god. Nobody's perfect. Only God is naturally good (Mark 10:18). The rest of us have sinned and fall short of the glory of God (Rom. 3:23).

Second, we know that humans cannot be inherently good because we have the facts of history. History is largely a record of man's inhumanity to man. Despite being the most educated and sophisticated generation ever, we still have wars, crime, violence, and prejudice. That is because the root of the problem is still present in us. We still selfishly seek our own way. History simply reflects the results of our actions.

The third reason I don't believe humans are inherently good is that I am a parent. If you are a parent, you know the idea that man is inherently good is a silly idea. I didn't have to teach my kids to lie. Did you? Of course not. It just comes naturally. I didn't have to teach my kids to be selfish. Nor did you. Humans have an innate tendency to do wrong. The Bible says so, history proves it, and parents know it is so.

Reason number four to refute the goodness of humans is the knowledge of my own heart. This may shock you, but the truth is that a lot of times I don't want to be good. In fact, a lot of times I like to sin! Sometimes I would rather be unloving than loving; I would rather return a smart remark than be patient. And sometimes I am just plain selfish. I do not like to do what is good, even when I know it is the right thing to do. I want to be lazy instead. And even when my desire is right, even when I want to do good, I still struggle to actually do it.

Do you struggle to do good, even when you *want* to do what is right? God says that this struggle is normal. "Can the Ethiopian change his skin or the leopard its spots? Neither can you do good who are accustomed to doing evil" (Jer. 13:23). It takes more than willpower to change your nature. You don't just snap your fingers and become a good person.

The apostle Paul found this to be true in his own life. Perhaps you can identify with him. I can. In Romans 7 Paul says that no matter which way he turns, he can't make himself do right. He wants to, but he can't. When he wants to do good, he does not, and when he tries not to do wrong, he does it anyway.

When we realize we are not perfect, we tend to comfort ourselves with comparisons: "Well, I may not be what I ought to be, but I am better than so and so." You have probably heard someone say that, or you may have even said it yourself. The only problem with this approach is that God does not grade on a curve. He does not judge us according to how we compare with other people. Jesus Christ is his standard of measurement, and he is perfect. That means that when we measure ourselves by Christ, we do not measure up. We all fall short.

It is like the little boy who came to his mother and said, "Mommy, I'm eight feet tall."

She said, "You are?"

"Yes," he insisted. "I'm eight feet tall."

His mother asked what he measured himself with, and he pulled out a six-inch ruler.

We must evaluate ourselves by God's perfect standard of goodness, Jesus Christ. When we do that, we realize the truth that no one is perfectly good.

Our Goodness Is a Gift from God

God did not save us because of our goodness but because of his own kindness and mercy. Thanks to the saving work of Jesus Christ our Savior, God can declare us good. Our goodness is a gift from God. We cannot work for it. We cannot earn it. We do not deserve it.

The Bible calls this work of Christ *justification*. That is a big word that simply means God says you are okay because of what Jesus did for you. When you put your trust in Christ, God gives you a new nature. (It is like starting over; that is why it is called being "born again.") Then God not only gives you the *desire* to do good, but also gives you the *power* to do good. Philippians 2:13 says, "It is God who works in you both *to will* and *to do* for His good pleasure" (NKJV, emphasis added). He gives you the *desire* and the *power* to do what is right. That is one of the ways you know you are a Christian.

By God's grace and power we are re-created as good people, and then we are given the ability to do good deeds. God works from the inside out, not from the outside in. He says, "Let me change you on the inside, and the outside will fall into place." Now, what does that mean? Does it mean that a Christian never sins? Of course not. All of us make mistakes. All of us sin. What it means is that now that I am a Christian, I have a new power and a new desire to do what is right. God solved the problem of my old selfish nature by giving me a new Christlike nature.

LEARNING TO DO GOOD

God has done the work of changing my nature. Now I need to cooperate with his efforts and work at letting his goodness fill me. Titus 3:14 says we must *learn* to do good. Here are five simple suggestions for learning to do good.

Master Your Bible

First, *become a student of God's Word*. Read the Bible, study it, and memorize significant portions of it. Fill your mind and your life with it. You have only two sources from which to develop your values—the world or the Word. The choice is up to you.

I was once given a new Bible, and the person who gave it to me wrote in the front of it: "This book will keep you from sin, or sin will keep you from this book." That's true. Paul writes in 2 Timothy 3:16: "The whole Bible was given to us by inspiration from God and is useful to teach us what is true and to make us realize what is wrong in our lives; it straightens us out and helps us do what is right" (LB). So master the Bible if you want to do good. Fill your life with it.

It is not enough to own a Bible; you have to use it. A Bible in the hand is worth two on the shelf. If I were to ask you if you believe the Bible from cover to cover, you would probably say you do. But have you read it from cover to cover? How do you know you believe it if you don't even know what is in it?

Some Christians are more faithful to Dear Abby than they are to God's Word. They are more faithful to the sports page. They wouldn't think of going to bed without reading the stock report. They devour the newspaper every day, but they go day after day without cracking open the Bible. And the Bible is what teaches us to know right from wrong.

Perhaps you are saying, "Well, Rick, I don't understand the Bible." The solution is simple: get a modern version. There are many good ones. Get the *Good News Translation* or the *Living Bible*. Get a good study Bible like the *New International Version Study Bible* or *The Life Application Bible*. When someone says, "I don't understand the Bible," I am reminded of Mark Twain, who said, "It's not the parts of the Bible that I don't understand that bother me, it's the part that I do understand." Do you find that to be true?

When I see a person whose Bible is falling apart, I discover that the person usually isn't. Master the Bible.

Guard Your Mind

Second, if you want to do good, you must *learn to control your thought life*. This is essential, because as a man "thinks in his heart, so is he" (Prov. 23:7 NKJV). Sin always starts in the mind. Satan plants ideas—called temptations—in your head. If you nurture these temptations in your mind, they will become visible in your life. Sin always starts in your mind, so guard your mind.

Most people are very careless about what they allow to enter their minds. I am amazed at what some Christians watch on TV. They say, "Oh, it doesn't bother me to watch that kind of stuff." Really? Jesus says in Matthew 6:22, "The eye is the lamp of the body. If your eyes are good, your whole body will be full of light." The next verse says, "But if your eye is clouded with evil thoughts and desires, you are in deep spiritual darkness" (LB). Psychiatrists, psychologists, and other experts now say that we never really forget anything. We may not remember it all consciously, but everything we have seen or heard is in our subconscious. It all gets mixed up in the mind, and that is why we have those crazy dreams. So guard your mind. Be discriminating. Don't let just anything come into your mind.

When you are bombarded with garbage on TV, you have a choice. You can change the channel, or better yet, you can turn off the set and spend some time in God's Word. If you want to do good, think about good, positive, and uplifting things—things that are true, honest, just, pure, lovely, and of good report (Phil. 4:8 KJV). Stop allowing poisonous material to enter your mind. If you want to do good, you have to be more careful about what you give attention to. Guard your mind.

Develop Convictions

Third, if you want to learn to do good, you must *develop some convictions*. What do you stand for? It has been said that if you don't stand for something, you will fall for anything. This is especially true in America's pluralistic society, where tolerance of opposing viewpoints is a prized virtue. We love to appear open-minded. The problem is that some people are so open-minded that their brains fall out! They don't stand for anything.

Do you know the difference between an opinion and a conviction? An opinion is something that you hold; a conviction is something that holds you. An opinion is something you will argue about. A conviction is something you will suffer for and, if necessary, die for.

Do you realize that Christians are supposed to hate some things? Romans 12:9 says, "Hate what is evil; cling to what is good." That is pretty clear: we are supposed to hate evil. Why? One reason is because of what evil does to people. Evil hurts and destroys people. When you take a close look at Jesus, you realize that goodness means standing for what is right and standing against what is wrong. He hates sin but loves sinners. We tend to do the exact opposite: we hate sinners and love sin. But God wants us to have both compassion for people and conviction against sin.

Goodness demands some gutsy conviction—taking a stand against things like child abuse, abortion, pornography, and corruption. I heard on the radio that one out of every four girls in America will be molested by the time she is eighteen. We have to take a stand against evil like that! Christians also need to speak up when someone takes the Lord's name in vain. When you hear about some dishonest activity, speak out against it. Philosopher Edmund Burke once said, "All that is necessary for the triumph of evil is that good men do nothing." Develop some convictions.

You need to realize, of course, that if you develop some convictions, you will not be popular with everyone. Some people will call you a fanatic or a religious nut. When that happens, remember that Peter says it is better to suffer for doing good than for doing evil (1 Peter 2:19–20). Jesus warns that the more we identify with him, the more the world around us will respond with hostility.

If you stand up for your convictions, you can count on opposition. The Bible says that in the last days there will be people who hate good (2 Tim. 3:3). Remember that Jesus Christ lived a perfect life, yet he was criticized, mocked, misunderstood, and eventually killed on a cross. So what makes you think life will be any easier for you? That leads us to the fourth step in learning to do good.

Muster the Courage to Be Different

To learn to do good, you must have the courage to be different from your culture. This is scary because American society pressures us to conform, to go with the flow. You have to "go along to get along." When you go to the office party, you are expected to act the way others do. We are all encouraged to act alike, talk alike, dress alike, and smell alike just to fit in. But sometimes goodness means being willing to stand alone. Dare to be different. As 3 John 11 says, "Do not imitate what is evil but what is good."

Do you remember the story of the three young Israelite men who wouldn't bow down to the statue of King Nebuchadnezzar and were thrown into the fiery furnace (Dan. 3)? When you are a person of integrity, you are going to go through the fire. You can count on it.

Speaking of heat, are you a thermostat or a thermometer? You are one or the other. A thermometer *registers* the temperature. It simply reflects its environment, whether it's hot or cold. A thermostat, on the other hand, *controls* the temperature. It influences its environment; it sets the standard. Which are you—a thermometer or a thermostat?

One of my favorite Bible verses is 1 Peter 3:11. The author writes of having a "passion for goodness" (Moffatt). Goodness means more than just avoiding evil. Goodness also means being enthusiastic for what is right. We should promote what is positive and good.

In Romans 15 Paul compliments the Christians in Rome. He says, "You ... are full of goodness" (v. 14). At that time Rome was the sin capital of the ancient world. It would make Las Vegas look like a Sunday school picnic. Every kind of debauchery and immorality you could think of was going on in Rome. And when in Rome, what are you expected to do? You are expected to do as the Romans do! But a certain band of people refused to indulge in such sinful behavior. They had integrity. Paul wrote to them, "In the middle of this cesspool, you are full of goodness." What a testimony! What a reputation! Wouldn't you like to have that kind of reputation?

Meet with Other Believers

Finally, if you want to do good, you must *develop the habit of meeting with other believers*. One secret of the Roman Christians' goodness is that they were good together. They met together regularly to challenge and encourage and support one another in their Christian lifestyle. The author of Hebrews tells us to "consider how we may spur one another on toward love and good deeds." Then he adds this important ingredient: "Let us not give up meeting together ... but let us encourage one another" (Heb. 10:24–25).

Our fellowship with other believers is designed to encourage us to live good lives in an evil world. As Christians we are not to imitate the world, but neither are we to live in isolation from it. Both extreme approaches to the world are wrong. Rather, we are to learn to live *in* the world without being *of* the world. That was Jesus' prayer for his followers in John 17. He prayed, "My prayer is not that you take them out of the world but that you protect them from the evil one" (v. 15). The answer is not imitation or isolation, but *insulation*. God *will* protect us from evil, and one of the most powerful means he uses to do that is the church.

You don't find soldiers going out on their own to do battle with enemy forces. They go in groups called companies or platoons or battalions. They know they need each other. Why then do so many Christians think they can go it alone in life? Don't they realize they are in a battle with spiritual forces of evil? (Eph. 6). Don't they recognize the dangers? I honestly think many Christians don't even know there is a war going on. They are so out of touch with spiritual realities that they don't recognize they are in the middle of a battle.

But Christians who know the score realize they need each other. They enjoy church gatherings as R & R from the front lines of battle. They see the worship service as a spiritual service station where they can get filled up and tuned up and prepared to go back to the battle.

Conclusion

The Christian life is not easy, but it is eternally worthwhile. And doing good is not always easy, but there is a reward. Galatians 6:9 says, "Let us not become weary in doing good, for at the proper time we will reap a harvest if we do not give up." How do you fight the weariness? How do you keep on keeping on? By mastering the Bible, by guarding your mind, by developing convictions, by having the courage to be different, and by meeting regularly with other Christians for support and encouragement.

Are you satisfied to be a thermometer, simply registering the spiritual coldness of the environment around you? Or are you willing to be God's thermostat in your corner of the world? Use your influence for God and for good in your world this week.

PUTTING THOUGHTS INTO ACTION

1. Based on what you have read in this chapter, how do you define a "good life"?
2. Of the five ways to learn to be good, which is the one you need to work on most at this time?

CHAPTER 9

THE ONE WHO CAN BE COUNTED ON

So far in our study of the fruit of the Spirit, we have looked at love, joy, peace, patience, kindness, and goodness. In this chapter we consider the quality of faithfulness. You may be saying to yourself, "I am not sure I can take on any more. I haven't mastered patience yet." Don't despair. Remember, you are growing the *fruit* of the Spirit—a set. All nine qualities are interrelated and grow together.

Faithfulness is a word we do not hear very often these days. It is a word usually reserved for retirement parties. After twenty-five years of faithful service, a worker gets a gold watch. When most of us think of the word *faithful*, we think of things that are old. My dog may be old and ugly, but he's faithful. My car may be old and ugly, but it's faithful.

To be faithful means to be reliable, trustworthy, dependable, consistent. Faithfulness is a rare quality. The Bible asks, "Who can find a faithful man?" (Prov. 20:6 NKJV). It is not easy to find someone who can really be counted on. The *Good News Translation* expresses Proverbs 20:6 this way: "Everyone talks about how loyal and faithful he is, but just try to find someone who really is!" As a pastor I have learned that not everyone who volunteers to serve actually comes through.

The first reason we should be faithful is that God is faithful. Psalm 33:4 says, "[The LORD] is faithful in all he does." Since God desires for us to be like him, he wants us to learn to be faithful. Moreover, faithfulness makes life easier. Unfaithfulness is the cause of many problems in life. Proverbs 25:19 says, "Like a bad tooth or a lame foot is reliance on the unfaithful in times of trouble." Unreliable people are a pain—like a bad toothache or a sore foot. You know what it is like to have a bunion or a corn on your foot. It hurts. When you are depending on an unreliable person, you can never quite relax. In the back of your mind you are always wondering, "Will he let me down again, or will he come through this time?" Working with inconsistent people is extremely frustrating.

We all look for faithfulness in others as we go about our daily activities. We want the paper carrier to be reliable so that we can read the newspaper at our accustomed time with our usual cup of coffee. We want the mail carrier to be faithful; when I mail a letter, I depend on the mail service to deliver it. I want the food at my favorite restaurant to be consistent from week to week.

The most famous geyser in America is Old Faithful at Yellowstone National Park. It is not the biggest geyser in America, nor is it the most powerful. What makes the geyser famous is its faithfulness! It runs like clockwork. Dependable. People appreciate dependability—even in a geyser.

Do you have a reputation for being reliable? Would those who know you well stake their lives on your faithfulness? You may be talented, educated, and creative, but if you are not dependable, your talents are not worth much. Someone has said, "The greatest ability is dependability."

Another reason why we should be faithful is that God rewards faithfulness. In the parable of the talents recorded in Matthew 25, Jesus says that one day God is going to judge us. But this judgment will not be to evaluate our ability or good intentions. God is going to judge us and reward us according to our faithfulness. The Bible says a faithful person will be richly blessed. So if you want to be rewarded in heaven, you should learn how to become a faithful, dependable person.

Let's look at eight things you can do to develop faithfulness in your life.

Keep Your Promises

Proverbs 25:14 says, "Like clouds and wind without rain is a man who boasts of gifts he does not give." Do you know people like that? They make promises but never keep them. They may say, "I am planning to do it," but they never get around to it.

Be careful about the promises you make. Have you ever told someone you would call back later and then didn't do it? Have you ever said, "The check is in the mail," before it was? Have you ever promised you would pray for someone and then forgotten to? You need to be dependable when you say, "I will return it soon" or "We will do it later." Keep your word!

Sometimes as a parent, in a moment of weakness, I make promises to my kids just to get them out of my hair. Do you ever do that? I promise them something that doesn't even register in my mind. Weeks later I may not remember what I said, but I have learned that my kids never forget anything. Never! When I say, "Well, we might, *maybe*, do something," they interpret my words to mean we are *definitely* going to do something. Start packing. You have to keep your promises.

Proverbs 20:25 says, "It is a trap for a man to dedicate something rashly and only later to consider his vows." In other words, it is always easier to get in than it is to get out. Do you know the number one problem in parent-child relationships? Resentment. And the number one cause of resentment is broken promises.

Ecclesiastes 5:5 says, "It is better not to vow than to make a vow and not fulfill it." Husbands, what promises do you need to keep? Have you promised to take your wife on a vacation, or have you promised to repair a leaky faucet or to help with a special project? What about your kids? Have you promised to spend more time together or to play baseball?

When you are dependable, you don't have to convince people that you are. You don't have to make a big deal of it. You don't have to say, "Cross my heart, hope to die, stick a needle in my eye." No, you just say you will do it, and then you do it! Jesus said to let your yes be yes and your no be no (Matt. 5:37). Over time, your track record will speak for itself. Others will feel confident that they can count on you. And God will be making careful notes in heaven.

HONOR YOUR MARRIAGE

In a wedding ceremony the bride and groom exchange rings as symbols of the vow they are making. They promise to be faithful to each other for the rest of their lives. They don't have to commit adultery to be unfaithful. All they have to do is let something else take priority over their marriage. This can be anything: sports, community or church activities, television, work. The Bible says that if you are married, your relationship to your mate is to be second only to your relationship to God. Hebrews 13:4 says, "Marriage should be honored by all." Circle that word *honored*. The word means "to hold in respect," "to value with high esteem," and "to take seriously."

If you want to develop the quality of faithfulness, honor your marriage. Put effort into it. The Love Chapter, 1 Corinthians 13, says that when you love someone, the person you love can count on you. Being loving and being dependable go hand in hand. On the flip side, when you are unreliable, you are not loving. Faithfulness is a choice. It is not dependent on what others do. You make a commitment, and regardless of what your mate does, you choose to be faithful to the vows you made before God. Keep your promises and honor your marriage.

Use Your Talents

God has given you some spiritual abilities, talents, and gifts. He has made an investment in you, and he wants and expects a return on that investment. "Each one should use whatever gift he has received to serve others, faithfully administering God's grace in its various forms" (1 Peter 4:10). If you do not use the talents you have been given, other people will be cheated because you are not contributing what God has uniquely equipped you to provide.

If you want to become more faithful, use your talents. You might say, "Well, I'm not talented like so and so. I can't sing the way she can." Just because you cannot do the spectacular, you are not excused from doing what you can. Faithfulness does not depend on what I do not have or cannot do. Faithfulness depends on what I do with what I have. I am not responsible to sing solos for God if he didn't give me that gift. But I am responsible to use the gifts and talents God has given me.

We cannot all be brilliant, but we can all be faithful. And faithfulness is what counts with God! So keep your promises, honor your marriage, and use your talents.

MAKE THE MOST OF YOUR TIME

Time is something we all have in common. Everyone has the same amount of time — 168 hours in a week. Ephesians 5:15 says, "Live life, then, with a due sense of responsibility, not as men who do not know the meaning of life but as those who do. Make the best use of your time" (Phillips).

You can do three things with your time — spend it, waste it, or invest it. The best use of your time is to invest it in something that is going to outlast you. Faithfulness involves time management.

There are two primary time wasters: regret and worry. When we regret the past, we waste huge amounts of time looking backward to change something we can't change anyway. When we worry about the future, we waste time fretting over events that may never happen. As a result, we waste the time and energy allotted for today. To become a more faithful person, you are going to have to give up what I call "*when* and *then* thinking." "*When* the kids start school ... *when* the kids finish school ... *when* the grandkids start school ... *when* I retire ... *when* we pay all the bills, *then* I will be able to serve the Lord." God says be faithful now.

Let me offer you a guilt-relieving statement: God understands your schedule. He really does. He understands it better than you do. So what should you do? Talk to him about it. Say, "God, tell me what I need to cut out. Tell me what I need to add." When you burn the candle at both ends, you are not as bright as you think you are. You probably need to cut out some things. You may need to add some other things. God can help you make these choices.

So make your time count. It is a part of being faithful.

STAND BY YOUR FRIENDS

Another way to develop your faithfulness is to cultivate personal loyalty. A faithful person stands by his or her friends. Proverbs 17:17 says, "A true friend is always loyal, and a brother is born to help in time of need" (LB). Genuine friends are reliable and consistent. They can be counted on in a crisis. Someone has said that when times get tough, a genuine friend doesn't see through you but sees you through. To whom are you loyal? Who can count on you? Do they know it?

A few years ago the associate pastor in the church I serve took me out to lunch, and as we sat down, he said, "I just want to say one thing. No matter what happens, I will always be your friend." Loyalty like that is a priceless treasure. You can't put a price tag on it.

If I asked you to write letters to five people you knew you could count on, to whom would you write? What if I turned it around? Who would write to you and say, "I know I can depend on you if things get tough"? Stand by your friends.

Manage Your Money

If you want to develop the fruit of faithfulness, you must learn to manage your money. God has given you resources, and how you handle money is a test of your faithfulness to him. Jesus says, "If you have not been trustworthy in handling worldly wealth, who will trust you with true riches?" (Luke 16:11). Amazing! God says that if you are not faithful with your material possessions, he will not trust you with spiritual resources. So you need to ask yourself questions, such as, "Am I faithful in tithing to the Lord? Do I pay my bills on time? When I compare my giving with my spending and my spending with my savings, is my life really in balance? Am I being a wise manager of the money God has given me?" The way you handle your finances determines to a large extent what God can do in your life.

What does it mean to be faithful with your finances? Specifically, what does it mean to be faithful in giving? First Corinthians 16:2 says, "On every Lord's Day each of you should put aside something from what you have earned during the week, and use it for this offering. The amount depends on how much the Lord has helped you earn" (LB). This verse defines what it means to be a faithful giver. It says three things.

First, we should give *regularly*. We are to give weekly, on every Sunday. A faithful person's giving is systematic, not spasmodic. It is not, "Oh, I feel good today. I am going to tip God. Here, Lord!" I used to think that the most spiritual giving occurred when a person was impulsively moved by emotion to give. Not true. God says giving should be consistent, *every* Sunday, whether we feel like it or not. And this principle relates to the second aspect of faithful giving.

God says your giving should be *planned*. You should prayerfully plan and set aside something from what you have earned. If you are married, you should sit down with your mate and discuss the amount you feel God wants you to give each week. If you don't plan it, you will not give consistently. Remember, God is looking for faithfulness. My wife and I have a tithe account. We have found that the only way we can be faithful in our giving is to keep a record of it. So we actually have a tithe account in our ledger. It is account Number One. Before we pay any bills, we return our tithe to the Lord. The ledger helps us to be faithful.

Finally, faithful giving is *proportional*. It is a percentage of your income. The amount you should give depends on how much the Lord has helped you earn. That is what tithing is all about. A tithe means 10 percent. Giving 10 percent should be the minimum—the starting point. If God has richly blessed you financially, you may be able to give much more than 10 percent. We are to give back to God a percentage of what he enables us to earn.

Do Your Best at Work

The seventh way to become more faithful is to do your best at your job. If you were responsible for hiring people at work, what would you look for? I imagine that one quality you would look for is dependability. During the time I have been a pastor, I think I have filled out a reference form on someone practically every week. I have never seen a reference form that doesn't mention dependability, trustworthiness, punctuality, reliability, or consistency. Employers, colleges, and mission agencies all want to know about a person's faithfulness in work habits.

How can your work affect your faithfulness? Jesus says, "Whoever can be trusted with very little can also be trusted with much" (Luke 16:10). Life is largely made up of little things, so if you are not faithful in the little things, you will not be faithful in most of life. The same thing is true of spiritual growth. The little things, such as having a daily quiet time and prayer, produce big results. Success comes from being faithful in the little things that other people may overlook.

Do you have a "guilt pile" at work? Most people do. It is that little stack of things you have not gotten around to yet. Faithfulness includes how you handle your guilt pile. It may not mean much to you that someone has written you a letter, but the writer of that letter expects an answer. His world may be depending on it. How do you handle the little things in life?

Faithfulness is also affected by how we handle what is not ours. Jesus says, "If you have not been trustworthy with someone else's property, who will give you property of your own?" (Luke 16:12). When I am at work, am I as trustworthy with the supplies as if I were paying for them? If I ran a business, would I be taking extra coffee breaks? If I rent a rototiller to use on my garden, do I take as good care of it as I would one I owned? Would I want to buy the rental car I just abused for a week? How do you handle things that are not yours? God says that is a test of faithfulness.

See how practical this is? Faithfulness is important in many areas of your life. That is why God says you are going to be rewarded for your faithfulness. Do your best at work. The Bible says, "Whatever you do, work at it with all your heart, as working for the Lord, not for men" (Col. 3:23). Christians ought to have a reputation for being the most dependable people at work. They are always aware of who their true boss is.

COMMIT YOURSELF TO A CHURCH

One more way you can develop faithfulness is to commit yourself to a specific, local body of believers. Paul writes in Romans 12:5, "In Christ we who are many form one body, and each member belongs to all the others." Each believer belongs to all the others in the body of Christ. That is why the local church is so important.

Christians are engaged in a spiritual battle (Eph. 6:10–18). Many of the words used in the Bible to describe the Christian life are war terms: *fight, conquer, strive, battle, overcome, victory.* Christians are likened to soldiers (2 Tim. 2:3). Paul tells us to "put on the full armor of God"

(Eph. 6:11). You are in a spiritual battle whether you know it or not, and you need support and reinforcement. When you became a Christian, you signed up to be a part of God's army.

Suppose I go to a recruiting office and say I want to join the army. They say, "Great, sign here on the dotted line." Then I say, "Well, wait a minute! I want to join the army, but I have one condition. I don't want to be committed to any specific platoon. I want to be able to float around from platoon to platoon. I'll be part of the army, but I don't want to be committed to a specific group of soldiers. If the battle gets a little hot in one area, I'll move to another area and join another platoon. And if I don't like one platoon's leadership, I'll join another platoon." Would you like to have someone like that fighting by your side in a foxhole? Of course not! Yet that is how many Christians today relate to God's army. They float around from church to church with little or no commitment to any specific group of Christians—so while the battle is being fought, they are AWOL.

When you became a Christian, you committed yourself to Jesus Christ. Now you can become a part of the local body of believers by committing yourself to those people. That is what "church membership" is—a commitment to other Christians. It is a decision to become a participant, not merely a spectator. You stop being a consumer and become a contributor.

Having traveled many places overseas, I have discovered that "free-floating" believers are a phenomena found only in America. Nowhere else in the world will you find people who claim to be believers but are not committed to a local fellowship.

I like what my wife said when someone asked her what the difference is between just attending church and becoming a member of one. She said, "It's like the difference between getting married and just living together. The difference is commitment."

Who can count on you? Can anyone? There is no such thing as a Lone Ranger Christian. *Koinonia*, the Greek word translated "fellowship" in the Bible, means being as committed to each other as we are to Jesus Christ. Jesus said, "By this all men will know that you are my disciples, if you love one another" (John 13:35). One way love expresses itself is in faithfulness to others.

CONCLUSION

Whether it is keeping your promise, honoring your marriage, being committed to your church, doing your best at work, or being loyal to your friends, God will honor your faithfulness. Why? Because he wants you to become more and more like Jesus Christ, who was faithful unto death.

You cannot overestimate the importance of faithfulness. Jesus told a parable about a master who went away and left his servants in charge (Matt. 25:14–30). When he returned, the servants were rewarded not for their ability, their knowledge, or their good intentions, but for their faithfulness. Jesus has left you and me in charge of his business here on earth, and one day he will come back. When he returns, will he find us faithful?

PUTTING THOUGHTS INTO ACTION

1. On a scale of 1 to 10, how would you rate yourself at this time regarding dependability and faithfulness (a) at home, (b) at work, and (c) at church?
2. What is a specific way by which you recently showed your loyalty to a friend?

CHAPTER 10

A Gentle
Approach

Everyone wants friends. Everyone needs friends. It is a medical fact that people who have friends live longer.

Years ago Dale Carnegie wrote the number two bestselling book of the twentieth century, *How to Win Friends and Influence People*. Why has it sold so many copies? Because everyone wants to be liked by others. We all want friends. Proverbs 18:24 says, "A man who has friends must himself be friendly" (NKJV). In other words, if you want to be liked by others, it helps if you are likable. And one of the most likable qualities is what the Bible calls "gentleness."

In the 1980s many people went to the movies and enjoyed watching tough characters like Dirty Harry and Rambo, but nobody really wants to live with those kinds of people. We want people around us to be understanding, kind, and gentle. What is gentleness? Based on the original Greek word used in the New Testament, the word *gentleness* literally means "strength under control." The word was used to describe a wild stallion that had been tamed or broken. The tamed stallion still had as much power and energy as when it was wild, but it could now be controlled and made useful for its master. To be gentle does not mean to be weak and wimpy. Interestingly, only two people in the Bible were called gentle—Jesus and Moses—and neither of them were weak men. Both were very strong, masculine men.

Galatians 5:23 lists the eighth fruit of the Spirit: gentleness. Philippians 4:5 tells us to "show a gentle attitude toward everyone" (GNT). Gentleness is controlling your reactions to people. It is *choosing* your own response to people rather than simply reacting to them.

In this chapter we consider how you can practice gentleness with six types of people with whom you come in contact all the time.

Be Understanding, Not Demanding

When someone *serves* you, *be understanding, not demanding*. Philippians 2:4 says, "Don't just think about your own affairs, but be interested in others, too, and in what they are doing" (LB).

How do you treat people who provide a service to you? How do you treat the restaurant workers, clerks, secretaries, employees, bank tellers, and others who serve you? Are you rude and demanding? Are you indifferent and impersonal as if they were just part of the machinery? Do you understand that they may have had a hard day too, or do you think only of yourself? The first way you can develop gentleness is to work at understanding the people who serve you.

The secret to getting great service at a restaurant is to treat those who serve you with respect. It is amazing how much more helpful servers are when you are considerate of their feelings and are sympathetic to the pressure they are under. Looking beyond your own needs and agenda takes a little effort, but the results are well worth it.

I read a popular self-help book once in which the author said that when you return defective merchandise, you should ignore the clerk and complain directly to the manager. While this approach may be effective, the author showed no respect for clerks by bolding proclaiming, "All clerks are jerks." That is being demanding instead of understanding.

The first place you can be gentle is at home. The Bible says that wives are to adorn themselves with "a gentle and quiet spirit" (1 Peter 3:4). That is more valuable than any clothes you can wear or any perfume you can put on. Gentleness is an attractive attribute for a woman. To husbands, the Bible says, "You husbands should try to understand the wives you live with" (1 Peter 3:7 Phillips).

Be understanding, not demanding toward people who serve you and toward the people with whom you live.

Be Gracious, Not Judgmental

When someone *disappoints* you, *be gracious, not judgmental*. Galatians 6:1 says, "If someone is caught in a sin, you who are spiritual should restore him gently. But watch yourself, or you also may be tempted." The temptation Paul is referring to in this passage may well be the temptation to be judgmental, to be "holier than thou." And that is the wrong response for a Christian to have toward a brother or sister in Christ who is struggling with sin. Romans 14:1 says, "Accept him whose faith is weak, without passing judgment on disputable matters." We set ourselves up for Satan's attack in our own areas of weakness the moment we begin to judge others.

What is your reaction to people when they mess up their lives? Do you secretly think, *I told you so* or *I could see it coming* or *It serves you right* or *How could you be so dumb*? Do you have an inward sense of superiority? Jesus' reaction to the woman caught committing adultery was full of sensitivity. He defended her in front of other people, and then, after the crowd had left, he dealt with her privately about her sin. He was gracious, not judgmental.

Why should we work at not being judgmental? Because that is the way Christ has treated us. Romans 15:7 says, "Accept one another, then, just as Christ accepted you, in order to bring praise to God." God puts up with a lot from us. And if he puts up with our inconsistencies and weaknesses, we can learn to put up with others' shortcomings. Whenever you feel tempted to judge another person, pause to remember how much God has forgiven you. The more you recognize God's grace to you, the more gracious you will be to others.

You will become gentler when you are understanding, not demanding, of the people who serve you. When people disappoint you, you will become gentler when you learn to act graciously toward them and not judge them. God is consistently gentle with you, and he wants you to be gentle with others.

BE TENDER WITHOUT SURRENDER

When someone *disagrees* with you, *be tender without surrender*. You will never be able to please everyone. You will always meet people who like to argue and quarrel with you. Some people will contradict everything you say. How should you respond to them?

One of the tests of spiritual maturity is how you handle people who disagree with you. Some people have a need to devastate everyone who disagrees with them. If you challenge them or offer a comparison, complaint, or criticism, they respond with a full-blown personal attack. Then what do you do? You have three alternatives: you can retreat in fear, you can react in anger, or you can respond in gentleness. Most people choose between retreating or reacting. Few know how to respond in gentleness.

If you give in and retreat in fear from argumentative people, you say, "Okay, have it your way." "Peace at any price" brings many hidden costs to any relationship.

On the other hand, if you react in anger, you take the offensive and fight back when someone opposes you. Anger is usually a telltale sign that you feel insecure and threatened by someone's disapproval. And anger is a warning light that tells you that you are about to lose something, often your self-esteem. When people become angry, their most common reaction is to become sarcastic and attack the other person's self-worth.

The third alternative—responding in gentleness—is the approach God wants you to take to opposition. This kind of response requires a fine balance between maintaining your right to an opinion while equally respecting another's right to his or her opinion. It requires being tender without surrendering your convictions.

Proverbs 15:1 says, "A gentle answer quiets anger, but a harsh one stirs it up" (GNT). I am sure you have found that to be true in your experience. It has been true in mine. When someone asks you a question, if you respond arrogantly, the questioner will probably challenge you. But if you respond quietly, the questioner will be more likely to be open to your answer. When you shout at people in a loud voice, they get very defensive.

James 3:16–17 says, "Where there is jealousy and selfishness, there is also disorder and every kind of evil. But the wisdom from above is pure first of all; it is also *peaceful*, *gentle*, and *friendly*" (GNT, emphasis added). James pinpoints the cause of quarrels and arguments: selfishness—wanting our own way and demanding that others agree with us. But he goes on to say that wise persons are peaceful, pure, gentle, and friendly. I know many people who are very intelligent, but they are also obnoxious. They know it all. They are not friendly, peaceful, or gentle. They go around trying to impress everyone with their knowledge. If you are a truly wise person, you are gentle.

I once read a book called *Patton's Principles: A Handbook for Managers Who Mean It*, a collection of short statements by Gen. George S. Patton of World War II fame. One of his principles is never fight a battle when you won't gain anything by winning. Do you ever fight those kinds of battles in your marriage? For instance, have you ever argued meaninglessly over a date?

"It was in 1982."

"No, it was 1983."

"No, it wasn't. It was 1982."

"No, it was . . ."

Who cares? Never fight a battle in which you won't win anything. Your relationship with your spouse is worth more than the point you are trying to prove. Maybe you and your spouse are at a dinner party and your mate starts telling a story. You say, "Now honey, it wasn't that way. Remember, it was Aunt Mary, not Aunt Sue." Do you think the other people listening care which aunt it was? No. Not at all. Don't let your ego get involved. Be wise. Be gentle.

Gentleness is the ability to *disagree agreeably*. You can walk hand in hand with someone without seeing eye to eye. Besides, if two people agree on everything, one of them is not needed.

Writing to Timothy, Paul said, "The Lord's servant must not quarrel; instead, he must be kind to everyone, able to teach, not resentful. Those who oppose him he must gently instruct, in the hope that God will grant them repentance leading them to a knowledge of the truth" (2 Tim. 2:24–25).

Paul is saying that gentleness is a qualification for spiritual leadership. If I am a leader, I am not to get swept into arguments. You and I are not to get involved in petty disagreements and pointless conflicts. Specifically, these verses say that pastors are to be gentle and instruct those who are in opposition to their leadership.

So far we have discussed three aspects of gentleness: be understanding, not demanding; be gentle, not judgmental; and be tender without surrender. You don't have to give up your convictions, but you do need to be tender in the way you express them. Let's look at a fourth aspect.

BE TEACHABLE, NOT UNREACHABLE

When someone *corrects* you, *be teachable, not unreachable*. James 1:19 says, "Let every man be quick to listen but slow to use his tongue, and slow to lose his temper" (Phillips). If you do the first two things, the third one naturally falls into place. If you are quick to listen and slow to answer back, you are going to be slow to lose your temper. Proverbs 13:18 says, "Whoever heeds correction is honored." If you want to be a gentle person, use your ears more than your mouth, and be willing to accept correction.

The Greek word translated "gentle" is sometimes translated "meek." I don't like that word because it, unfortunately, rhymes with *weak*. People tend to equate meekness with weakness. What do you think of when you hear the word *meek*? Probably a doormat. Maybe you imagine a picture of the old cartoon character Caspar Milquetoast, the self-effacing comedian Pee-wee Herman, or a little kitten cowering in a corner. Yet Jesus called himself "meek" (Matt. 11:29 KJV), and he certainly was not afraid of anyone. Moreover, Jesus said, "Blessed are the meek, for they will inherit the earth" (Matt. 5:5). The meek—the gentle—will inherit the earth because they are God's kind of people; they are like Jesus Christ.

The wisest people I know are the people who have a "teach me" attitude and are willing to learn from others. I have discovered that I can learn from anyone. You can too if you just know the right questions to ask. It is important that you never stop asking questions, because the moment you are through learning in life, you are through! Be teachable, not unreachable.

From whom are you willing to learn? Husbands, can you learn from your wife, or does that threaten you? When your wife comes to you and makes a suggestion, do you get defensive? Do you take every comment as a personal threat to your manhood? (Or maybe you are the opposite, as with the wife who said to her husband, "Are you a man or a mouse? Now squeak up!")

Wives, can you learn from your husband, or does that threaten you? Can you learn from your children? I have learned a lot from my kids.

If you want to end up lonely in life, never admit your mistakes. Never learn from anyone. Never let anyone teach you anything. I guarantee that you will end up being a very lonely person. Nobody has all the answers. I do not. You do not. No one does. So we must all keep on learning. Consider the man who was a witness in court. The bailiff said, "Do you swear to tell the truth, the whole truth, and nothing but the truth, so help you God?" The man answered, "Sir, if I knew the whole truth and nothing but the truth, I would be God!" That is true. None of us has all the answers. Gentleness involves being willing to learn from others.

Gentleness is also being willing to admit when you are wrong. How long has it been since you admitted to your spouse, "Honey, I was wrong.

It was my fault"? Some people haven't said that in years.

James 1:21 says this willingness to learn is also the attitude we should have when we come to God's Word: "Humbly accept the word planted in you." The Greek language uses the same word for "humble" and "gentle." It is also the word used for "meekness." It means to be teachable, not unreachable. When we approach God's Word, we ought to approach it with a gentle, or humble, attitude that says, "God, I am willing to be taught."

BE AN ACTOR, NOT A REACTOR

When someone *hurts* you, *be an actor, not a reactor.* By "actor" I don't mean hypocrite or pretender, but one who *initiates* action. The apostle Peter recalled how Jesus acted at his trial before Pilate. "When they hurled their insults at him, he did not retaliate; when he suffered, he made no threats. Instead, he entrusted himself to him who judges justly" (1 Peter 2:23). While Pilate was questioning him, Jesus could have commanded all the angels in heaven to come down and rescue him in an instant. The trial was not even legal. But Jesus endured the trial in silence.

Who was really in control of that situation: Pilate or Jesus? The psychological dynamics of that confrontation are fascinating. Pilate was threatened by the simple fact that Jesus wouldn't speak up and defend himself. It made Pilate nervous. Rather than react to Pilate, Jesus assumed control of the situation by choosing to remain silent. He didn't need to react to Pilate's insults because he knew exactly who he was—the Son of God.

When someone hurts you, be an actor, not a reactor. Strength is found in gentleness. And gentleness is the ability to handle hurt without retaliating. It is the ability to absorb the blow without striking back. Jesus called it "turning the other cheek." You say, "That's not easy to do." No, it's not; it is almost impossible. "To respond that way is not natural," you say. You're right. It is supernatural; it is the fruit of the Spirit. You need God's power to live this way.

When someone at work stabs you in the back, what do you do? Do you pull out your big guns and react? Maybe you say, "You make me so mad!" When you say that, you are admitting that someone else is controlling your emotions. You are acknowledging that you have given that person the power to determine your feelings and reactions. Remember this: no one can *take* that control from you. You give it away the moment you start reacting. If someone is unfaithful to you, do you react by being unfaithful to that person? Learn to be an actor, not a reactor.

God's Word tells us, "Do not repay anyone evil for evil.... Do not be overcome by evil, but overcome evil with good" (Rom. 12:17, 21). That is the power of action rather than reaction. To retaliate is to react. To forgive is to act. It is saying, "I choose the way I respond."

Syndicated columnist Sydney Harris tells of accompanying a friend to a newsstand and watching him greet the salesman very courteously. In return, however, he received gruff, discourteous service, as the salesman rudely shoved the newspaper in his direction. Harris's friend politely smiled and wished the man a nice weekend. As they walked on down the street, Harris asked his friend, "Does he always treat you so rudely?"

"Yes, unfortunately, he does."

"Are you always so polite and friendly to him?"

"Yes, I am."

"Why are you so nice to him when he's so unfriendly to you?"

"Because I don't want him to decide how I'm going to react."

That is gentleness. That is strength under control—choosing the way to respond to people. That is choosing to be an actor rather than a reactor.

Do you let other people control your emotional state? Do you let people raise your happiness level or plunge you into worry, fear, or anger? Proverbs 16:32 says, "He who is slow to anger is better than the mighty, and he who rules his spirit than he who takes a city" (NKJV). The person who can control his moods is stronger than an army in a city that has a wall around it. But a person who cannot control his own spirit is defenseless, like a city with no walls around it. You have no defense; you are at the mercy of whatever anyone wants to do to you. (We say more about this in the next chapter when we look at the fruit of self-control.)

Be Respectful

There is one last type of person with whom you should practice gentleness: unbelievers. When you witness to people, when you share your faith, *respect them, don't reject them*. Have you noticed that a lot of evangelism is just a thinly veiled put-down? Some share the gospel with a sense of superiority: "You need what I have because you're so bad." People do need the Good News, but our attitude can keep them from receiving it. Respect unbelievers; don't put them down. Respecting them means accepting them. That does not mean that you must approve of their lifestyle. There is a difference between acceptance and approval. I can accept you as a person of worth without approving of everything you do. And I must honor your right to be treated in a respectful way.

First Peter 3:15 says, "Always be prepared to give an answer to everyone who asks you to give the reason for the hope that you have. But do this with *gentleness* and *respect*" (emphasis added). The manner in which you share the gospel can determine how willing a person is to listen to you. In fact, your attitude speaks more powerfully than the words of your message. Unfortunately, some people use the gospel as a sledgehammer.

There are two ways to get an egg out of an eggshell. One way is to crack it open; the other way is to put it in a warm, loving environment and let it incubate and hatch. The second way preserves the baby chick while the first way kills it. Likewise, there are two ways to get the Good

News across to people. You can pound them over the head with it, or you can love them into the family of God. The most effective way to share the gospel with unbelievers is to surround them with love and acceptance as you share the gospel with them. Be gentle. Respect them, don't reject them. Theologian D. T. Niles said, "Evangelism is just one beggar telling another where to find bread."

Jesus was gentle, and he wants us to be gentle in telling others about him. Gentleness was natural to Jesus, but it doesn't come naturally to most of us. We must learn to be gentle.

CONCLUSION

One of the positive benefits of becoming gentler is a more relaxed lifestyle. You will become more adaptable, more able to roll with the punches. One reason many people experience emotional burnout is that they are not gentle. They are always demanding their rights. They judge others. They always have to prove their point. They are unwilling to learn from others. They react to situations, usually in anger or fear. And they seldom treat others with respect or dignity.

Now do you see just how important gentleness is for a healthy and happy life? Take stock of your life for a few minutes. In which relationships do you find it difficult to be gentle? Be specific. Write down your problem areas and put the list in your Bible. Then, as you are reading the Word and praying, talk to God about those relationships and ask him to help you be gentle with those people. Remember, you cannot do it by yourself, no matter how much willpower you have. Gentleness is a fruit of the Spirit.

PUTTING THOUGHTS INTO ACTION

1. Explain the difference between being wrongfully judgmental (this chapter) and being helpfully straightforward (chapter 7).
2. What is one way you have shown yourself to be teachable?

CHAPTER 11

DEVELOPING SELF-CONTROL

Many of your problems and mine are caused by a lack of self-control. Why can't I lose weight? Why can't I hold on to a job? Why can't I keep the house clean? Why can't I get more done? Why can't I break that bad habit? Why can't I get out of debt? I can't do these things because I need self-control. My biggest problem is me!

Perhaps, like many people today, you feel that your life is out of control—and maybe it is. You feel overwhelmed by circumstances and pressures. You feel defenseless and vulnerable. Like a car with a broken steering wheel, you screech around curves with no sense of control over the steering. That is a scary feeling. Proverbs 25:28 says, "Like a city whose walls are broken down is a man who lacks self-control."

Self-control brings with it the good feeling of competency. Like a finely tuned precision automobile, your life stays on course with the slightest touch of steering. The results of self-control are confidence and an inner sense of security.

Self-control and self-discipline are also key factors in any success you hope to have in this life. Without self-discipline you are unlikely to achieve anything of lasting value. The apostle Paul realized this when he wrote, "Every athlete in training submits to strict discipline, in order to be crowned with a wreath that will not last; but we do it for one that will last forever" (1 Cor. 9:25 GNT). "No pain, no gain" is the way fitness trainers put it, and they are right. Peak performance requires self-discipline and self-control. Olympic athletes train for years to have a chance to win a brief moment of glory. But the race we are running is far more important than any earthly athletic event. So self-control is not optional for Christians.

If we are to achieve true freedom, we need self-control. The Greek philosopher Epictetus was right when he said, "No man is truly free until he masters himself." Jesus expressed the thought in these words: "Everyone who sins is a slave to sin" (John 8:34). Samson may have been the strongest man in the world, but he was enslaved by his lusts and desires because he lacked self-control. Strength without self-control got him into trouble.

People will try almost anything to gain self-control, or to make up for the lack of it. Pills, therapy, seminars, resolutions, surgery—people try them all. One advertisement for a weight-loss program had this heading: "If you've never succeeded at losing weight permanently, maybe you need a little inside help." I thought, *Great! That's right up my alley. The Bible says to be strong in the inner man—inner control.* So I read on:

> You're fed up with weight loss programs, right? You've tried nearly every one, only to put the weight right back on. Well, there's something you should know. Overeating is not just a bad habit. It's a disease. And like any other, you can't treat it on your own. You need professional help. You can get it from [Are you ready for this?] the *Gastric Bubble Program....* Here's how it works. A plastic bubble is inserted into your stomach without surgery. Two things happen. It takes up a large space, causing you to

eat less. And decreases your appetite. *The result: You lose weight.*[1]

As I said, people will try almost anything to gain more self-control—or to make up for their lack of it.

Well, if "quick and easy" answers don't bring self-control, how do we get it? God's Word is quite clear on this subject. Let me suggest seven steps to self-control.

Admit Your Problem

The first step in developing self-control is to *accept responsibility for your lack of self-control*. Admit your problem. James 1:14 says, "A man's temptation is due to the pull *of his own inward desires*, which can be enormously attractive" (Phillips, emphasis added). This verse says that we do things because we *like* to! When I do something I know is bad for me, I still do it because I like to do it. I want to do it. It's an inner desire.

We often try to ignore our problems or deny we have them: "What problem? I don't have a problem." We often rationalize, "It's just the way I am" or "Everybody else is doing it." Sometimes we blame others: "If I just had different parents" or "The devil made me do it." We can blame anyone, but as long as we waste our energy fixing the blame, we cannot fix the problem.

James says we like to take the course of least resistance, and giving in to temptation is usually that easiest course. The starting point for developing self-control is to face what God has already said: We are responsible for our behavior.

Do you want more self-control? The first step is to admit that you have a problem and be specific about it. "I have this problem. This is where I need help." You may have a problem with food, drink, words, your temper, money, exercise, sex, TV, clothes, time—all these areas need self-control. Begin praying specifically about your problem areas.

Put Your Past behind You

The second step in developing self-control—and this is very important—is to *put your past behind you*. Paul says in Philippians 3:13–14, "Forgetting what is behind and straining toward what is ahead, I press on toward the goal." This passage exposes a misconception that will keep you from gaining self-control: once a failure, always a failure. You may say, "Oh, I tried to quit my bad habit.

In fact, I have tried fifteen times. I guess I will never be able to get control of this." That is a misconception.

Failure in the past does not mean you will never be able to change. Focusing on past failures, however, does guarantee their repetition. It is like driving a car and looking in the rearview mirror the whole time. You are going to collide with what's ahead of you. You have to put your past behind you.

Have you watched a baby just learning to walk? She may fall down a lot, but she doesn't stay down. She keeps on trying, and ultimately she succeeds. A baby learns to walk by persistence. Can you image where you would be if you had given up when you tripped and fell two or three times? *It's hopeless. I'm a failure. I'll never be a walker. Let's just face it—some people are meant to be walkers, and some people are not meant to be walkers. I just know I'm not meant to be a walker because I have tried and failed three times.*

The first time I kissed a girl, I was very nervous. I mean, I didn't want us to bump noses. So I sort of turned my head a little bit, and she turned her head a little bit, and we aimed for a connection. I am embarrassed to admit what happened next. She had long hair, and my glasses got caught in her hair. My first kiss was a fiasco. But I'm so glad I didn't give up on kissing!

Put your past behind you. It doesn't matter how many times you have failed. Try again. Only this time try a new way, admitting you have a problem. When Thomas Edison was developing a new invention, he would repeatedly run into problems and find that the thing just didn't work right yet. He had to try again. He once said, "Don't call it a failure, call it an education! Now you know what doesn't work!"

Talk Back to Your Feelings

The next step in becoming more self-controlled is to *talk back to your feelings*. Challenge them. We put far too much emphasis on our feelings today. We think everything has to feel good or it is not worthwhile. "I don't feel like studying." "I don't feel like working." "I don't feel like getting out of bed." "I don't feel like reading my Bible." "I don't feel like washing the car." Or, on the flip side: "I feel like another helping of food." "I feel like having another drink." "I feel like watching TV for ten hours." "I feel like sleeping until noon." Don't give your feelings so much authority. Feelings are highly unreliable.

Do you let your moods manipulate you? God doesn't want you to be controlled by your feelings. He wants you to master your moods. With Christ as the Master of your life, you *can* learn to master your feelings. Talk back to them. God says he wants you to learn how to challenge your emotions.

For instance, let's say you are fighting the battle of the bulging waistline. Before you ever walk into the kitchen and open the refrigerator door, you have begun to talk to yourself about eating. If you are serious about losing weight, you will have to challenge some of those subconscious attitudes about food. When you hear your mind saying, *I just have to have a snack or I'll die*, you will have to talk back to yourself and say something like, "No, I'm not going to die if I don't eat a snack. In fact, I will be healthier if I don't."

Titus 2:11 – 12 says, "For the grace of God ... teaches us to say 'No' to ungodliness and worldly passions, and to live self-controlled, upright and godly lives." God's grace gives you the power to do what is right. God gives you the ability to say no to that feeling, to that desire, to that impulse.

With God's supernatural help, you can master your moods.

BELIEVE YOU CAN CHANGE

If you are going to change and become more self-controlled, you have to *start believing you can change*. Your beliefs do control your behavior. In almost every chapter of this book, I have mentioned that the fruit of the Spirit begins in your thought life. The seed must be planted in your mind. The way you think determines the way you feel, and the way you feel determines the way you act.

The person who says, "I can't do it," and the person who says, "I can do it," are both right. Much of the time you set yourself up to be defeated by a habit by saying, "I could never stop this. It's just the way I am. I will never be able to change." Your belief becomes a self-fulfilling prophecy.

Three times in 1 Peter, God reminds us to be clear-minded and self-controlled. Why? Because a clear mind has a lot to do with self-control. God gave us the power to change our habits when he gave us the power to choose our thoughts. Does Romans 12:2 tell us to be transformed by working hard or by sheer willpower? No. What are we to be transformed by? The renewing of the mind.

When your self-control is being tested, you need to fill your mind with the promises of God. Let's look at one of God's beautiful promises.

First Corinthians 10:13 says, "God is faithful; he will not let you be tempted beyond what you can bear. But when you are tempted, he will also provide a way out so that you can stand up under it." If you are a Christian, you cannot ever say, "The temptation was too strong; I couldn't help myself." The Bible says God is faithful. If you are a Christian, he will not let you be tempted beyond what you can bear. He never puts more *on* you than he puts *in* you to bear it.

So focus on God's positive promises of help and strength. Philippians 4:13 says, "I can do all things though Christ who strengthens me" (NKJV). You can change. You can be different. Stop setting yourself up for failure by constantly criticizing yourself. Stop nagging, condemning, and putting yourself down: "Oh, I'm worthless. I'm no good. I shouldn't even go to church. I simply have no control over my life." Nagging doesn't work—on yourself or on anyone else! Instead, remember that Jesus says, "Everything is possible for him who believes" (Mark 9:23).

MAKE YOURSELF ACCOUNTABLE

The fifth step in developing your self-control is a tough one: *make yourself accountable to someone.* We may not like this step, but we desperately need it. Find someone who will check up on you, will pray for you, and will encourage you in the areas where you want to develop more self-control. Ecclesiastes 4:12 says, "Two people can resist an attack that would defeat one person alone" (GNT). That is the value of the Alcoholics Anonymous approach—the "buddy system"—in which you are encouraged to call someone whenever you feel the pressure building to return to old, destructive ways. Galatians 6:2 says, "Share each other's troubles and problems, and so obey our Lord's command" (LB).

Try this exercise. If you are serious about self-control, find someone in your church and go to that person and say, "I have this problem. I have confessed it to God. I have asked forgiveness, and now I want to ask you to help me. Will you be my 'buddy,' a person I can call on the phone when I need support and encouragement?" I believe God intends for every church to be filled with "buddy" relationships in which people are accountable to each other, relationships in which people help and encourage one another in the Lord. Having someone hold you accountable is tough, but it works.

What should you look for in a "buddy"? Several things. First, your buddy should be the same gender as you. When two people share their struggles, a natural bond of closeness develops and leads to intimacy. You don't need to place another temptation in your path by sharing personal problems with someone of the opposite sex. Second, you should look for someone you can depend on to follow through on this commitment—someone who is faithful. And look for someone who will keep your problem confidential. Do not choose someone who is known to talk too much. Finally, tell your buddy that he or she has permission to check on you from time to time. Give him or her the right to ask you, "How are you doing with your problem?" Knowing that someone will be asking you about your problem is an additional incentive not to give in to temptation. That may be the extra push you need to get you moving on the road to victorious self-control.

Avoid Temptation

The sixth step to becoming more self-controlled is plain common sense: *avoid the things that tempt you*. Stay away from situations that weaken your self-control. If you do not want to be stung, stay away from the bees.

As a youth director, I used to tell kids, "At this stage in your life your sexual drive is so powerful that you must be prepared in advance to control it. When you go on a date, you will be guided either by your plans or by your glands! So plan what you will do and won't do on the date. The time to begin to think about exercising self-control is not in the backseat of a car."

Plan in advance to avoid situations that you know are going to cause temptation in your life. Don't keep candy in the cupboard if you are trying to diet. Don't acquire credit cards if you are an impulsive spender. Plan your life to avoid the things that weaken your self-control.

Ephesians 4:27 says, "Don't give the Devil a chance" (GNT). Don't give him a foothold in your life. I once talked to a man who had quit smoking, and I asked him how he succeeded. He said, "I wet my matches!" In the time it took him to try to light a cigarette, he was back in control.

What in your life do you need to avoid? What do you need to get rid of? Some magazines? Some books or videos in your home? Maybe you need to break off a relationship you know is bad for you. First Corinthians 15:33 says, "Bad company corrupts good character." You may need to stay away from some people if every time you are around them you give in to temptation. Avoid both people and situations that tempt you to forfeit self-control.

A wonderful children's book entitled *Frog and Toad Together* by Arnold Lobel teaches a powerful lesson about the insufficiency of willpower. The following is from a section called "Cookies":

> Toad baked some cookies. "These cookies smell very good," said Toad. He ate one. "And they taste even better," he said. Toad ran to Frog's house. "Frog, Frog," cried Toad, "taste these cookies that I have made."
>
> Frog ate one of the cookies. "These are the best cookies I have ever eaten!" said Frog. Frog and Toad ate many cookies, one after another. "You know, Toad," said Frog with his mouth full, "I think we should stop eating. We will soon be sick."
>
> "You are right," said Toad. "Let's eat one last cookie, and then we will stop." Frog and Toad ate one last cookie. There were many cookies left in the bowl. "Frog," said Toad, "let's eat one very last cookie and then we will

stop." Frog and Toad ate one very last cookie. "We must stop eating," cried Toad as he ate another.

"Yes," said Frog, reaching for a cookie, "we need will power."

"What is will power?" asked Toad.

"Will power is trying hard *not* to do something that you really want to do."

"You mean like trying *not* to eat all of these cookies?" asked Toad.

"Right," said Frog. Frog put the cookies in a box.

"There," he said. "Now we won't eat any more cookies."

"*But* we can open the box," said Toad.

"That is true," said Frog. Frog tied some string around the box. "There," he said. "Now we will not eat any more cookies."

"*But* we can cut the string and open the box," said Toad.

"That is true," said Frog. Frog got a ladder. He put the box up on a high shelf. "There," said Frog. "Now we will not eat any more cookies."

"*But* we can climb the ladder and take the box down from the shelf and cut the string and open the box," said Toad.

"That is true," said Frog. Frog climbed the ladder and took the box down from the shelf. He cut the string and opened the box. Frog took the box outside. He shouted in a large, loud voice, "HEY, BIRDS. HERE ARE COOKIES." Birds came from everywhere. They picked up all the cookies in their beaks and flew away.

"Now we have no more cookies to eat," said Toad sadly. "Not even one."

"Yes," said Frog, "but we have lots and lots of will power!"

"You may keep it all, Frog," said Toad. "I'm going home to bake a cake."[2]

Toad's willpower is about as strong as that of some of us! My point is this: what in your life do you need to "feed to the birds"? What do you need to avoid? You may need to change your job because a relationship there is wrong and is harming you. That is a drastic measure, but you may need to do something that drastic in order to avoid whatever is tempting you at this particular time. You know you are not strong enough to resist it.

Let's review the steps for developing self-control that we have discussed so far: admit your problem, put the past behind you, talk back to your feelings, start believing you can change, make yourself accountable to someone, and avoid the things that tempt you. There is one more step, and it is the secret of lasting self-control.

DEPEND ON CHRIST'S POWER

If you want to develop self-control, learn to *depend on Christ's power to help you.* Galatians 5:16 says, "Let the Spirit direct your lives, and you will not satisfy the desires of the human nature" (GNB). The sequence in this sentence is very important. Let the Spirit direct your life—that's the first part—and you will not satisfy the desires of the human nature. Notice, it does not say you won't have those desires. Spirit-filled people are still going to *have* the desires of the flesh. It's just that you won't satisfy them.

We usually get the sequence backward. What we usually say is, "I am not good enough to have God's Spirit in my life. I am not worthy to have him direct me. My life is a mess. Once I get my act together, once I get this habit under control, then I am going to come to God and really live for him. Then I am going to let the Holy Spirit control my life."

By contrast, God says, "No, that's not the sequence." He doesn't say, "Get your act together and *then* I will help you." Rather, he says, "Let me into your life. Let my Holy Spirit control you *while* you are still struggling with that problem. I will help you change." The sequence makes all the difference.

What would you think if I said, "I am going to get well first, and then I am going to go see the doctor." You would say I was crazy. It is a ridiculous idea. "I am going to feel better, then I will take the medicine." It is absurd, but I hear people say things like that all the time. "You know, Rick, I'm gong to break this bad habit and then start attending church. I am going to clean up my life, and then I will commit it to Christ." Or, "I have a problem in my life, and I am going to wait until that problem is resolved, and then I will be baptized." The truth is that you need Christ in your life *now* to help you get over the problem. He has the power to help you change.

I have also heard many people say, "I am not good enough to be a Christian, so I am not even going to try." Fine! Don't try—just trust. Put your trust in Christ and depend on him to change what you have been unable to change. And find a church where you can grow. The church is a hospital for sinners, not a hotel for saints. The church is for people who are hurting. The church is for people who don't have it all together but are honest enough to say, "We're not perfect, but we want to grow. And we are all in this together."

Perhaps you say, "I know where I lack self-control, and I know that what I am doing is wrong, but I still like doing it." So what? Do you think that surprises God? The Bible says there is pleasure in sin for a season (Heb. 11:25). What does that mean? It means sin is fun—at least for a while. None of us would sin if sin immediately made us miserable.

Philippians 2:13 says, "For God is at work within you, helping you want to obey him, and then helping you do what he wants" (LB). God not only gives you the *desire* to do right, but also gives you the *power* to do what is right. Yet you must have him in your life first.

Conclusion

In what areas of your life do you have a hard time saying no? Is it hard for you to say no to food? To excessive spending? Alcohol? Drugs? Illicit sex? Cigarettes? Do you have trouble saying no to your feelings? Maybe you are really struggling with an addiction. Maybe nobody else knows about it—but the Lord does. And he cares about you. The best part is that he is able to do something about it.

The secret of self-control is Christ's control. If you have not yet done so, ask him to take control of your life right now. Then, as you face temptations that are too strong for you to resist, remember that he is with you and turn them over to him. Remember, Christ provides the power to change your life.

PUTTING THOUGHTS INTO ACTION

1. What is one area of your life where you need to develop self-control?
2. What specific action will you take to make yourself accountable in that matter?

CHAPTER 12

A PRODUCTIVE
LIFE

Have you ever wondered why some people are able to accomplish so much with their lives? What makes them so productive? In America we are very conscious of productivity at all levels. Once a month the government releases a report on our gross national product. It tells us how productive our businesses and industries have been. It is an important picture of our national economic health.

Suppose each of us were issued an "individual productivity report" each month. How would yours look? Would it show positive or negative results? Growth or decline? Think about the future. What do you want to do so that at the end of your life you will be able to say, "I led a productive life. I accomplished what I set out to accomplish"? Have you ever defined what you consider to be a productive life? More important, do you know God's definition of a productive, fruitful life? What does it mean to be a fruitful Christian?

The word *fruit* is used sixty-six times in the New Testament. Three different kinds of fruit are mentioned: the kind we eat—figs and grapes; biological fruit—babies; and spiritual fruit—Christlike character. In the preceding chapters we have looked at the fruit of the Spirit: love, joy, peace, patience, kindness, goodness, faithfulness, gentleness, and self-control. God wants to see that kind of fruit in our lives. That is his definition of a productive life.

In John 15:8, Jesus says, "This is to my Father's glory, that you bear much fruit, showing yourselves to be my disciples." The proof that you are a disciple is that you bear fruit. "You did not choose me," Jesus goes on to say, "but I chose you and appointed you to go and bear fruit—fruit that will last" (v. 16). God wants us to bear fruit—much fruit. He wants us to be productive. In this final chapter we look at the four conditions for fruitfulness that are described in the Bible.

CULTIVATE ROOTS

If we want to be fruitful, we must *cultivate some roots*. God says that without roots there will be no fruit. Jeremiah 17:7–8 says, "Blessed is the man who trusts in the LORD, whose confidence is in him. He will be like a tree planted by water that sends out its roots by the stream. It does not fear when the heat comes; its leaves are always green. It has no worries in a year of drought and never fails to bear fruit." If you don't have good roots, you simply won't bear any fruit.

This passage gives one reason why we need roots: to make it through tough times — times of heat and drought. Roots are the lifeline of nourishment for the entire plant or tree. Have you ever felt the heat in life — times when the pressure was on? That is when you need roots.

I grew up near the giant redwoods in northern California. Amazingly, the redwood trees there can withstand major forest fires. Because of their tremendous roots, they can even survive with four- or five-foot gashes in their trunks. Or consider a more common tree like an oak. If you were to place the roots of a large oak tree end to end, they would stretch out several hundred miles. That is why oak trees are so stable.

I read some time ago about the banana tree. It is almost indestructible. You can chop it into little pieces, but it will grow back. You can burn it down, but it will grow back. There is only one way to get rid of a banana tree, and that is by uprooting it. The roots are the key to the fruit.

Proverbs 12:3 says that "the righteous cannot be uprooted." Righteous people can stand the heat. They can also endure a time of drought, a long season without rain. In a drought, resources are limited. Everything dries up, and many things die. But the righteous endure.

Have you learned that sometimes in life you have to do without things on which you normally depend? You may be going through a drought right now. Maybe you are doing without emotional support. You are lacking friends or good health or a job or financial stability. Or you are trying to get by on limited time, energy, or money. How do you handle the dry spells in life? Do you wilt? Do you dry up and blow away?

If you ever visit the Arizona desert, you will find that it is full of different kinds of vegetation.

The contrasts have always fascinated me. The dried-up, brittle tumbleweed blows everywhere. Why? Because it has no roots. By contrast, the saguaro cactus bears fruit even in 130-degree weather. Why? Because the saguaro cactus has roots that go out fifty to sixty feet in all directions. You have to have roots if you are going to make it through a dry spell.

Anyone can survive a day of drought, but surviving an extended time of stress is another matter. For instance, if the cash flow in your business is bad for a month, you will probably say, "Well, we'll make it up next month." But by the end of the second month, if things don't pick up, you will begin to get a little anxious. By the third month you will start to panic, and by the fourth month you will probably fight major depression—unless you have some roots.

How do you cultivate roots? A good place to begin is by memorizing Psalm 1:2–3. The psalmist talks about the stable life, the life that has roots. He says roots are developed by reading and meditating on God's Word. We learn the same thing in the New Testament, in Colossians 2:6–7. Spend time daily reading, meditating on, memorizing, and obeying God's Word. That's how you develop strong spiritual roots, roots that go deep into the soil of God's Word. These roots will enable you to withstand the heat of pressure and the deprivation of drought.

ELIMINATE WEEDS

The second thing you need to do to be productive is to *eliminate the weeds* in your life. Jesus illustrates this in the parable of the soils. He mentions four kinds of soil, each representing one of the ways we can respond to God's Word. In Luke 8:11, 14 we read, "The seed is the word of God.... The seeds that fall among [weeds] stand for those who hear; but the worries and riches and pleasures of this life crowd in and choke them, and their fruit never ripens" (GNB). If you want to bear fruit, you have to cultivate good roots and then eliminate the weeds.

Here is a trivia question for you: How many kinds of weeds grow in the United States? The government reports 205 varieties of weeds in America. I estimate that 72 percent of those are in my back yard. In fact, I have thought about opening an exhibition and charging admission: "Warren's Weed Farm."

What are the weeds in your life? Many different types of weeds can crowd into your life and choke the spiritual vitality out of you. Weeds are the concerns and interests that sap your time, energy, and money and prevent you from bearing spiritual fruit.

People tell me, "I just don't have time to serve the Lord. I'm too busy. I don't have time to get involved." If that is true in your life, then you are too busy! You need to do some weeding. Many things in life are not necessarily wrong; they just are not necessary. Maybe you need to cut back your schedule a bit and eliminate the weeds.

Jesus mentions three varieties of weeds. Weeds of *worry* are a preoccupation with everyday cares and concerns that causes you to take your eyes off Jesus. Weeds of *riches*, a fixation with making money to buy more things, may dominate your life so much that you do not have time for the Lord. And weeds of *pleasure*—chasing "the good life"—can choke out your spiritual growth. It is fine to have a good time, but you need to guard your priorities. When the beach becomes more important than the Bible, your priorities are out of balance.

Consider this: how much effort does it take to grow weeds? What do you have to do to cultivate them? Nothing! They grow very well on their own. That is why they are weeds. You have to nurse your tomato plants, but you don't have to do anything to grow dandelions. They will grow—and grow rapidly—with no help from you or anyone else.

Weeds are a sign of neglect. When you neglect Bible reading, prayer, and fellowship with other Christians, weeds will grow up and choke your spiritual life, preventing you from bearing fruit. So if you are going to bear fruit, you have to deepen and cultivate your roots, and you have to eliminate the weeds in your life.

COOPERATE WITH GOD

If you are going to be a fruitful Christian, you must *cooperate with God's pruning* in your life. In John 15:1–2, Jesus says, "I am the true Vine, and my Father is the Gardener. He lops off every branch that doesn't produce. And he prunes those branches that bear fruit for even larger crops" (LB). Pruning involves *cutting off* the dead branches and *cutting back* the living branches, both to shape the tree or vine and to stimulate growth.

I have a neighbor who is an expert rose grower. His front and back yards are beautiful, so I invited him to come over to my back yard and work his magic on my roses. He was a wonder to watch. He brought his loppers to do his pruning, and he was ruthless. It hurt me just to watch him cut back my rosebushes. *Whack, whack, whack!* By the time he was finished, my rosebushes were only little stubs. Professional pruners will tell you that most people are too timid when it comes to pruning. I used to think that pruning was going in and gently cutting off the little dead pieces. Not so. The live stuff needs to go too—branches, leaves, and flowers. Evidently my neighbor knew what he was doing, because my roses have never bloomed so beautifully.

Here is my point: most of us think that when God prunes us, he cuts off the sinful and the superficial, the deadwood in our lives. He does do that, but he also cuts off stuff that is alive and successful: a business that is going great, a satisfying relationship, good health. Some of that may get whacked off for greater fruitfulness. It is not just deadwood that goes. God often cuts back good things too, in order to make us healthier. It is not always pleasant, but pruning is absolutely essential for spiritual growth. It is not optional. Remember, God is glorified when we bear "much fruit" (John 15:8), and that requires pruning. We must remember that the loppers are in the hands of our loving God. He knows what he is doing, and he wants what is best for us.

If you are a Christian, you are going to be pruned. Count on it. You may be going through pruning right now, and it may not all be dead-wood. God cuts off branches that we feel are productive so that more fruit may be produced. This can be confusing. We believe that we are being fruitful and are puzzled, even frustrated, by God's pruning. We ask, "Why are you doing this, God? I have given my business to you, but it's failing. I have committed my health to you, but I'm going into the hospital next week. I have been tithing faithfully, yet I'm going bankrupt."

I watched an educational TV program on houseplants in which the specialist suggested that viewers talk to their plants to help them grow. He explained that soothing, stroking, and talking to your Creeping Charlie will build the plant's self-esteem. Imagine yourself saying, "You're a good plant. My, you're looking good today! You look marvelous." Now imagine yourself talking to a plant you are pruning: "This hurts me more than it hurts you." *Whack!* "You'll thank me for this later!" *Whack!* "It's for your own good!" I can imagine the plant talking back, "You have no heart. You don't love me. I've worked long and hard to produce those roses you just cut off."

Isn't that what we say to God when he prunes us? "Don't you love me? Don't you care? Don't you see what's going on?" And we think God is angry with us. No, he's not angry. One of the biggest mistakes Christians make is confusing pruning with punishment. Pruning is not punishment, so don't equate the two. God is not angry with you. He just sees that you are someone who can bear more fruit, someone who has potential for greatness, someone he wants to use in a significant way. He wants you to be as fruitful as you possibly can be, so he prunes you back, even lopping off some of the things he has been blessing in your life. You lost your job? Don't worry. God has a better idea. He sees what you do not see.

How does God prune us? He uses problems, pressures, and people. Oh, does he use people! People will criticize and challenge you. They will question and doubt you. They will challenge your motives. God is using them to prune you. As I have said throughout this book, God can use every situation in your life to help you grow if you will just have the right attitude. He can use it all—the problems you bring on yourself, a major disappointment, a financial reversal, a sudden illness, a broken marriage, a rebellious child, the death of a loved one. He will and he does use them all as part of the pruning process to make you even more fruitful.

Why does God do this to us? Look at Hebrews 12:11: "No discipline seems pleasant at the time, but painful." We can all agree with that. It is not pleasant when you are being disciplined. The writer of Hebrews continues, "Later on, however, it produces *a harvest of righteousness and peace* for those who have been trained by it" (emphasis added). God does this for our own benefit as well as for his glory.

Like discipline, pruning is unpleasant. Have you ever looked at a pruned tree or a pruned plant? It is ugly. A few years ago I had twelve sixty-foot eucalyptus trees in my front yard. I had a man come out and top them. He "topped" them all right—he left no branches! I ended up with twelve "totem poles" standing in my front yard. Some of my neighbors joked that a UFO had dropped these giant toothpicks. I think some of them thought I was starting some kind of Stonehenge cult. Those trees were ugly. But do you know what? After that pruning, the trees came back with greater fullness than ever before. Now my problem is raking up all the leaves!

Pruning is never fun, and it is not pretty, but it is for your future benefit. The purpose of pruning is positive. God is not mad at you. The Bible says that there is "no condemnation for those who are in Christ Jesus" (Rom. 8:1). God does not "punish" his true children. Your punishment was taken care of on the cross. God's pruning is for your very best, for greater fruitfulness in your life.

My wife went through a time of severe pruning several years ago. She was ill, had a tough pregnancy, and was bedridden for months. It was a very tough time for our family. God cut back every activity in Kay's life. I mean everything—leading women's ministry, teaching Bible studies, all the things she loved and looked forward to doing. Even at home everything was chopped off; she couldn't get out of bed to do anything. We talked about it a lot because it didn't make sense at the time. Our church was growing rapidly, and I needed Kay's help. Nevertheless, it was a valuable pruning time. Kay learned a lot, because when you are flat on your back, all you can do is look up. Her fruitfulness in the years since has been astounding. God has opened up new ministries and opportunities for her that we never imagined. The results of that pruning in her life are exciting, but it wasn't fun going through it.

Can God's pruning fail to produce? Sure it can, if we don't cooperate. If we resist, rebel, complain, or become resentful, our character will not develop the way God intends it to. We have now looked at nine specific character qualities that God wants to develop in your life: love, joy, peace, patience, kindness, goodness, faithfulness, gentleness, and self-control. He produces these qualities by allowing you to encounter situations and people full of exactly the opposite qualities. He teaches you love by putting you around unlovely people. He teaches you joy in the midst of sorrow. He teaches you peace by allowing irritations all around you. He teaches you patience by allowing things to frustrate you. God uses all of those things to make you more fruitful, but you must cooperate with him. The way you express that cooperation is by praising God in every circumstance (1 Thess. 5:18).

WAIT FOR THE HARVEST

If I want my life to be fruitful, I must cultivate good roots, eliminate the weeds, and cooperate with God's pruning by thanking and praising him. I must also *wait for the harvest*. Growth takes time; it is not instantaneous. God takes two days to make mushrooms, but he takes sixty years to make an oak tree. Do you want to be a mushroom or an oak tree? Growth takes time.

When you examine your spiritual growth, you may wonder, *Why is it taking me so long to get better? I have been a Christian for two years, and I don't see much change. I am still struggling with my many weaknesses. Why?* Because spiritual growth, like natural growth, takes time. The best fruit ripens slowly.

Notice what Jesus says in John 12:24. He was talking about his death, but the principle he states applies to us as well. He said, "Truly, truly, I say to you, unless a grain of wheat falls into the earth and dies, it remains alone; but if it dies, it bears much fruit" (RSV). When Jesus says, "Truly,

truly," he means, "Now get this! Tune in! Listen and listen well. This is really important."

The point Jesus stresses here is that death precedes life. Just as a grain of wheat must die to produce fruit, so must we die to ourselves to produce spiritual growth. And dying to our own selfishness takes time. Our tendency is to dig up the seed periodically to check on its progress instead of trusting God to do his work in our lives. Christ will produce fruit in our lives if we remain in him. In the passage on the vine and the branches in John 15, the key word is *remain*. Remember that word. Remaining in Christ means keeping in contact with him, depending on him, living for him, and trusting him to do *his* work in our lives in *his* perfect timing. Never give up. It is always too soon to quit! Wait for God's promised harvest and, in the meantime, enjoy his presence in your life. God is pleased with you at every stage of your spiritual growth. He is not waiting until you are perfect to begin loving you. He will never love you any more than he already does.

As you look back over the chapters in this book, are you seeing spiritual fruit in your life? Perhaps you have memorized the ninefold fruit listed in Galatians 5:22–23. If not, I encourage you to do so. Think about how these qualities could be seen in the life of Jesus, and count on him to produce them in you by the working of his Holy Spirit. If you are not seeing as much fruit as you would like, don't despair. Remember that growth takes time. I recommend that you commit yourself to focus on one specific fruit of the Spirit each month for the next nine months. Use that month to study it in detail. Chapter 3 of the book *Rick Warren's Bible Study Methods* explains step-by-step how you can do a personal Bible study on a character quality.[1]

CONCLUSION

The four activities outlined in this chapter are the practical steps you need to take if you are serious about a fruitful, productive Christian life. Begin cultivating deep roots by spending time in God's Word every day. Then eliminate the weeds in your life that eat up your time and energy and distract you from doing God's will. Next, cooperate with God in the pruning process by thanking and praising him for what he is doing in your life. He is working to make you more fruitful than you ever thought possible. Finally, wait expectantly for the harvest of spiritual fruit in your life. If you have followed the first three steps, the harvest is inevitable!

In 1968 a scientist discovered a six-hundred-year-old seed necklace in an Indian grave. He planted one of the seeds, and it sprouted and grew. Although the seed had been dormant for six hundred years, it still had the potential for life. Maybe you have been a Christian for years and have been spiritually dormant for most of that time, but now you would like to be productive. You desire to be fruitful. Your reading this book is evidence of that. I have good news for you: it's not too late! You can begin right now. Bow your head in prayer and tell God you want to cooperate with his growth plan for you. He will provide the power to change your life.

PUTTING THOUGHTS INTO ACTION

1. What are some specific weeds that need to be pulled out of your life?
2. Give an example of God's pruning in your life.

BIBLE TRANSLATIONS

The following versions of the Bible are cited in this book:

Scripture quotations marked GNT are from the *Good News Translation — Second Edition*. © 1992 by American Bible Society. Used by permission.

Scripture quotations marked KJV are from the King James Version of the Bible.

Scripture quotations marked LB are from the *Living Bible*, copyright © 1971. Used by permission of Tyndale House Publishers, Inc., Wheaton, Illinois 60189. All rights reserved.

Scripture quotations marked Moffatt are from James Moffatt, *A New Translation of the Bible, Containing the Old and New Testaments*. New York: Doran,

NOTES

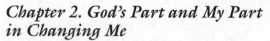

Chapter 2. God's Part and My Part in Changing Me

1. Viktor Frankl, *Man's Search for Meaning* (New York: Washington Square Press, 1997), 12.

Chapter 5. Peaceful Living in an Uptight World

1. Corrie ten Boom, *The Hiding Place* (New York: Guideposts, 1971), 177.

Chapter 6. Developing Your Patience

1. *Encyclopaedia Britannica 1982 Yearbook*.
2. Meyer Friedman and Ray H. Rosenman, *Type A Behavior and Your Heart* (New York: Fawcett, 1974).

Chapter 7. Putting on a Little Kindness

1. James Dobson, *Love Must Be Tough* (reprint, Sisters, Oreg.: Multnomah, 2004).

Chapter 11. Developing Self-Control

1. Advertisement in the *Orange County Register*, April 18, 1985.
2. Arnold Lobel, *Frog and Toad Together* (New York: Harper & Row, 1979). Used by permission.

Chapter 12. A Productive Life

1. Rick Warren, *Rick Warren's Bible Study Methods* (Grand Rapids: Zondervan, 2006), chap. 3: "The Character Quality Method of Bible Study."